la shirley audre nina
nus anna * ella emmy * emil
ypatia madonna a ben
sojourner * louisa sarah p
louise helen * mary * julia
cha * jos ann *
gari isadora * marsha artem
simone angelina junko ka
ilma yay vi
gertrude a er
frida * bea forugh juana
n * emily benazir artemisia
katya minerva anne g
irley audre nina amelia

THE LITTLE BOOK

of

FEMINIST SAINTS

JULIA PIERPONT

Illustrated by **MANJIT THAPP**

RANDOM HOUSE

NEW YORK

Published in the United States by Random House, an imprint and
division of Penguin Random House LLC, New York.

RANDOM HOUSE and the HOUSE colophon are registered trademarks
of Penguin Random House LLC.

Hardback ISBN 978-0-399-59274-4
Ebook ISBN 978-0-399-59275-1

Printed in China on acid-free paper

randomhousebooks.com

2 4 6 8 9 7 5 3 1

First Edition

Book design by Elizabeth A. D. Eno

For the women who brought us up,
and for the friends who've become women with us

CONTENTS

INTRODUCTION

I can't remember a time I was a child without also being a girl, a time I was a person before also being a female person. My mother told me a story about boys and girls, one that's taken on the weight of allegory for me: It was the summer before I turned four, and I was enrolled in a preschool called Magical Years. On a parent-chaperoned trip to the playground, my class put together a game of Peter Pan. My mother, with her long dark hair, was cast as Captain Hook. The moment the game began, the boys closed in, thwacking her as high up as their short arms could reach. The girls fled, yelling, "Chase me, chase me!" My mother was a diligent diarist in those years, and I asked her to look up her record of this day: "The girls want to taunt me and have me chase them; the boys want to hit me and kill me and eat the parts." How, she wondered, had this happened? My mother went to college in the seventies; she worked, she was part of a generation of women who had fought to break down the barriers of traditional gender roles. Insidious, they'd seeped in anyway.

This is a book about women who flouted those roles, thank god, because the world would be a lot worse off if they hadn't. Comprising a hundred women, our list is by no means complete. We—my editor, Caitlin McKenna, and I—began by compiling a few handfuls of names, those of women who had inspired and challenged us. Then we crowdsourced. My friend Jennifer Rice, in Austin, nominated Shirley Chisholm, the first black woman elected to the United States Congress—"Her campaign button said CHISHOLM: READY OR NOT because she didn't give a damn"—and forty-fifth governor of Texas Ann Richards, "who appointed women to everything." When

Manjit Thapp came on board as our illustrator, she put forth such candidates as Japanese artist Yayoi Kusama and gay-rights activist Marsha P. Johnson. Caitlin got her friends and colleagues at Random House to contribute a terrific variety of names as well. Katharine Hepburn got five independent nominations, and Marie Curie eight. When the list had swelled to four hundred, we began the disagreeable task of winnowing it down. The hundred women who remain come from all over the world, ranging as far back in time as the Greek poet Sappho, born c. 630 B.C., and as far forward as Pakistani activist Malala Yousafzai, born in 1997.

So why, then, is this *The Little Book of Feminist Saints*, when the women within encompass all religions, or sometimes no religion at all? The idea came from the Catholic saint-of-the-day book, the kind one might read as a source of daily inspiration throughout the calendar year. Each woman in the book is assigned her own feast day, so that, for example, one might read about the banana-skirted Josephine Baker on June 3, the day of her birth. On Valentine's Day, we celebrate Sappho and her poetry of desire. May 20 is for Amelia Earhart, who began her transatlantic solo flight on that day in 1932. Traditional Catholic saint books come with a complicated history. I happened upon an account of one such book of saints while reading about Queen Elizabeth I, a Protestant ruler in a previously Catholic country. When the dean of St. Paul's gave her the gift of a prayer book with pictures of saints, she rejected it. "You know I have an aversion to idolatry," she told him. I would argue that all the women in this book have done something with their lives that makes them worthy idols. So let this be the little, secular book of feminist saints.

These entries are not meant to serve as short biographies, summaries of each woman's life that could just as easily be found online. I tried, instead, in my daily research, to zero in on the colorful, the anecdotes I would find myself repeating to a friend that night. Connections began to emerge among the women as well. Some links were indirect: at the Chicago World's Fair in 1893, while Mary Cassatt's feminist mural *Modern Woman* was causing a stir within the exhibition, Ida B. Wells was just outside, boycotting the fair's omission of the African American community. As time went on, and the world got smaller, there were occasions of direct support among them. When Gloria Steinem's *Ms.* magazine debuted, in 1972, featuring a petition titled "We Have Had Abortions," the first lady of tennis, Billie Jean King, was among its fifty-three signees. When Ruby Bridges—who, in 1960, became the first African American child to attend an all-white Louisiana school following *Brown v. Board of Education*—was reunited, thirty-six years later, with her first-grade teacher, it was on a talk show helmed by the Queen of All Media, Oprah Winfrey. I had the feeling of stumbling upon a great sisterhood.

There is another entry in my mother's diary, written a month earlier: It was an unusually warm day in February, and we were at the schoolyard, playing Peter Pan then, too. "I was Captain Hook," my mother wrote. "Julia was Michael and John, Gabriella the crocodile, Lindsay was Wendy, and tiniest Antonia, whom we met there, was Pan." What is remarkable about this entry, apart from my mother's meticulously recorded cast list, is that there were no boys in the group that day, and so, like water, we girls filled the new space we'd been given. The women in these pages made and filled their own spaces—very often, *big* spaces—frequently when they hadn't been afforded any at all.

THE LITTLE BOOK OF FEMINIST SAINTS

ARTEMISIA GENTILESCHI

MATRON SAINT OF ARTISTS
B. 1593, ITALY
Feast Day: January 1

The judge ordered them to use thumbscrews, to ensure that the victim was telling the truth. There were gynecological exams in court, to confirm that her virginity had been, as she claimed, taken from her. The trial dragged on for eight months, during which time Artemisia never wavered from her testimony: Agostino Tassi, a painter her father had hired to act as her tutor, had raped her. In the end, Tassi, who'd been accused of rape before, was given a one-year sentence that he was never made to serve, and Artemisia was married off, quickly and quietly, and sent away, to Florence, where her real life's work began. She could neither read nor write, but she could paint. And she did paint: powerful women, women seeking revenge. Her best-known work, *Judith Slaying Holofernes*, depicts the Old Testament story of the widow Judith decapitating the general Holofernes, with remarkable violence. But it was her own face she used for Judith, and for the face of Holofernes, she painted Agostino Tassi's. It is the work for which he is remembered now, a man who was meant to be her tutor, and instead became her subject.

MICHELLE OBAMA

MATRON SAINT OF LADIES
B. 1964, UNITED STATES
Feast Day: January 17

We will never have a democracy until we have democratic families and a society without the invented categories of both race and gender. Michelle Obama may have changed history in the most powerful way—by example.

—Gloria Steinem

She went to a magnet school an hour and a half from her home, made the honor roll every year, graduated as salutatorian. But she still remembers the college counselor who told her, "I'm not sure if you're Princeton material." She was warned that she was overreaching, that the schools she was applying to were "too much" for her. "Then I got there and I looked around and thought: I'm just as smart as these people," she recalled. Smarter, it would seem. She graduated cum laude and went on to Harvard Law. When she met her future husband, at the law firm where they both worked, it was as his mentor; twenty years later, he would be sworn in as president. "Any First Lady, rightfully, gets to define her role," Ms. Obama has said. "There's no legislative authority; you're not elected. And that's a wonderful gift of freedom." Obama used her freedom to support military families, to combat childhood obesity (an issue that—despite rates having tripled in the twenty years before her husband took office—she knew would be "pooh-poohed as a sort of soft swing at the ball"), and to improve education across the United States, particularly for disadvantaged girls. "Kids are watching us," she said. "They're influenced by people they look up to, but it makes us want to live right and do right and be right—Every. Single. Day.—so that we don't ever disappoint these kids and they have something to hold on to, and so that they know—as I say all the time—I can *do* this. *You* can *do* this."

KANNO SUGAKO

Rise up, women! Wake up! As in the struggle workers are engaged in against capitalists to break down the class system, our demands for freedom and equality with men will not be won easily just because we will it; they will not be won if we do not raise our voices, if no blood is shed.

—Kanno Sugako

At first, she used her words. Kanno Sugako—Suga to her friends, the daughter of a miner, born in Osaka—ran the local paper after the original publisher was put in jail. "Women in Japan are in a state of slavery," she wrote. "We have been seen as a form of material property." When the government sought to shut down that paper, she started new ones. In 1908 she attended a socialist-anarchist rally and saw its leaders thrown in jail. The protest had been a peaceful one; the authorities beat her friends. It was then that Suga recognized the need for "an act of violence that would shake the entire nation to its symbolic foundations." When the plot to assassinate Emperor Meiji was uncovered, in 1910, twenty-six anarchists were put on trial. Suga was the only woman. "I shall die without whimpering. This is my destiny," she said in her final statement in court. "I shall die as one of the sacrificial victims. I have no regrets." In the diary she kept before her hanging, it is clear that she never lost her spirit: "If I could return as a ghost, there are so many people, beginning with the judge of the Court of Cassation, that I would like to terrify. It would be wonderful to scare them witless and make them grovel."

VIRGINIA WOOLF

MATRON SAINT OF WRITERS
B. 1882, ENGLAND
Feast Day: January 25

On a crisp October morning at "Oxbridge," a woman crosses the grass. She has had an idea that excites her, and she is lost in thought. A man intercepts her: only scholars may walk along the turf; women are to stay on the gravel path. The woman complies, and the man moves on. It is a small moment, but the woman has lost her train of thought. She goes to the campus library, wanting to see a manuscript of Thackeray's. But when she opens the library door, another man is there to meet her: women are not admitted unaccompanied. It is this series of refusals that would become the inspiration and opening to *A Room of One's Own*, the feminist rallying text that explored two "unsolved problems": women and fiction. Virginia Woolf, who owned and operated Hogarth Press with her husband, Leonard, recognized her unique privilege as a woman with artistic freedom. "I'm the only woman in England free to write what I like," she observed. Woolf's toughest battle was with her own mind, with the mental illness that eventually drove her to take her own life before the age of sixty. "We cannot, I think, be sure what 'caused' Virginia Woolf's mental illness," wrote biographer Hermione Lee. "We can only look at what it did to her, and what she did with it. What is certain is her closeness, all her life, to a terrifying edge, and her creation of a language which faces it and makes something of it." Her diaries reveal a mind unremittingly engaged. In an entry from 1927, while she was working on *To the Lighthouse*, Woolf wrote, "My brain is ferociously active. I want to have at my books as if I were conscious of the lapse of time; age and death."

OPRAH

MATRON SAINT OF EVERY HOME
B. 1954, UNITED STATES
Feast Day: January 29

The Oprah Winfrey Show was the number one talk show in America, averaging 12.6 million viewers every single weekday, when its thirty-seven-year-old star put taping on hold to fly east to Capitol Hill. There, she testified before the Senate Judiciary Committee regarding the establishment of a national database of convicted child abusers. "I am committed to using all of my will to follow through on this legislation," she told the committee. "I intend to make this my second career." Indeed, she had personally hired an attorney to draft a plan for such a registry. Much has been made of Winfrey's enormous wealth, as well as her generosity (and penchant for sending her audiences home with free cars), but here was a cause of greater personal significance. Winfrey herself is a survivor of childhood sexual abuse, having been raped on multiple occasions, beginning at age nine—by an uncle, a cousin, and a family friend. It is something she discussed openly on her show, which pioneered a uniquely confessional new format. She connected with audiences because she knew people, and she let them know her. After Winfrey's testimony in D.C., the committee chairman—and future vice president—Joe Biden told her, "I look forward to your announcement to run for public office." In 1993, two years after Oprah's testimony and thirty years after she was first raped, President Clinton signed the National Child Protection Act. They called it the Oprah Bill.

DEL MARTIN AND PHYLLIS LYON

MATRON SAINTS OF MARRIAGE
B. 1921 AND 1924, UNITED STATES
Feast Day: February 12

*We would never have marriage equality in California if
it weren't for Del and Phyllis.*

—NANCY PELOSI

The first time Dorothy "Del" Martin and Phyllis Lyon were married, it was February 12, 2004. Theirs was the first same-sex wedding in San Francisco, allowed under orders from Mayor Gavin Newsom. Six months later, the union was voided by the California Supreme Court.

The second time Martin and Lyon were married, it was four years later, after the court reversed its decision, legalizing same-sex marriage in California. They wore the same pantsuits they had at their first wedding. Once again, they were first in line.

By that time, they had been a couple for fifty-six years. Together they had founded the Daughters of Bilitis, the first political organization for lesbians in the United States, and edited *The Ladder*, the first nationally distributed lesbian publication in the country. "We were fighting the church, the couch, and the courts," Martin recalled. "Nothing was ever accomplished by hiding in a dark corner. Why not discard the hermitage for the heritage that awaits any red-blooded American woman who dares to claim it?" Their second marriage lasted only two months; Martin died in August 2008. "I am devastated," Lyon said in a statement, "but I take some solace in knowing we were able to enjoy the ultimate rite of love and commitment before she passed." Seven years later, when the U.S. Supreme Court declared same-sex marriage legal across the country, Lyon, age ninety, said, "Well, how about that?" She laughed and laughed. "For goodness' sakes."

FOROUGH FARROKHZAD

MATRON SAINT OF FREE VOICES
B. 1935, IRAN
Feast Day: February 13

She was divorced and wrote about the joys of sex ("a sin all filled with pleasure"). She was an Iranian woman and wrote about the repression that came with that ("Seek your rights, Sister"). She bought cheap paper in bulk, writing thousands of lines she never published. What she did publish earned her a reputation as Iran's Sylvia Plath. "I never saw her in a state of not being productive, she was like that," said filmmaker Ebrahim Golestan, her former lover, fifty years after her untimely death (a car accident when she was thirty-two). Farrokhzad described her poetry as "a vital need, a need on the scale of eating and sleeping, something like breathing." Born in Tehran, she traveled to Europe to "be a woman, that is to say 'a human being.'" But she always came back. At the time of her death, she was planning to perform the title role in a Persian translation of George Bernard Shaw's *Saint Joan*, in Tehran. "I love our Tehran, in spite of everything," she wrote. "I love it and it is only there that my life finds a purpose and reason...those heavy sunsets, those dirt roads, and those miserable miscreant corrupt people I love."

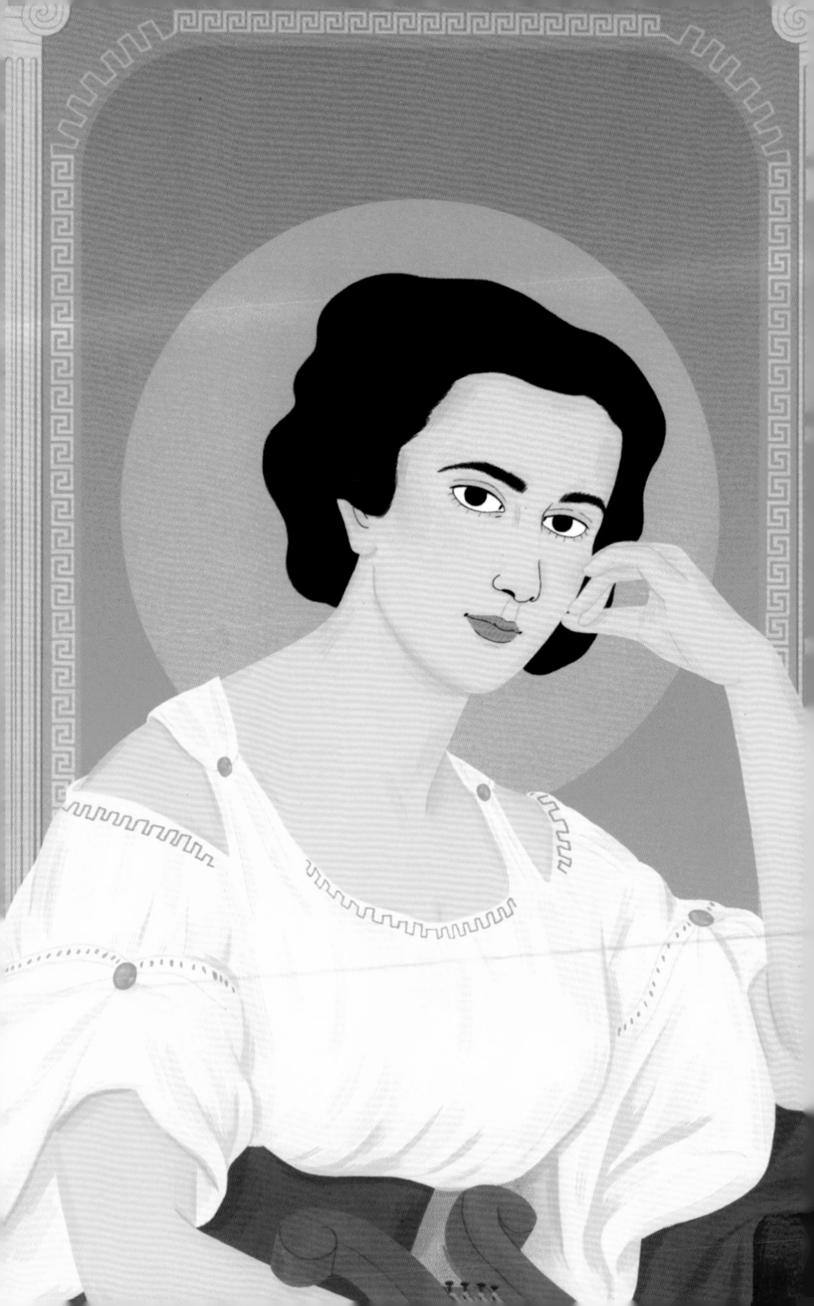

☀ SAPPHO ☀

MATRON SAINT OF LOVERS
B. 630 B.C.E., GREECE
Feast Day: February 14

He seems to me an equal of the gods—
whoever gets to sit across from you

—SAPPHO, translated by Daniel Mendelsohn

Plato called her "the Tenth Muse." The early church declared her "a sex-crazed whore who sings of her own wantonness." Though only a fraction of Sappho's lyric poetry survives today, her significance, both then and now, cannot be overestimated. In 300 B.C.E., King Seleucus I sent for a doctor to diagnose his son, the crown prince Antiochus. Young Antiochus's heartbeat was irregular, he fainted, and the color would suddenly fade from his skin. It was observed that his condition became apparent only in the presence of his stepmother, Stratonice. Thus the doctor concluded that Antiochus was suffering from erotic infatuation—because the symptoms were "as described by Sappho"—and Seleucus divorced his wife, giving way for his son to marry her. In modern times, Sappho, who wrote about loving men and women, has served as an icon for lesbian women, with philosopher and gender theorist Judith Butler stating that, as a queer teenager, "As far as I knew, there was only me and a woman called Sappho."

BARBARA JORDAN

MATRON SAINT OF THE CONSTITUTION
B. 1936, UNITED STATES
Feast Day: February 21

Your mother rides the bus all the way from Houston to Washington, D.C., to see you sworn in. The first woman, the first African American to be elected to Congress from Texas. *The Washington Post* would later call you "the first black woman everything." The day of the swearing-in, you wear black, with a white orchid. This becomes a sort of uniform for you, black with white. You don't mind the extra attention. You would stand out anyway. For your skin, for your sex—most of the other women in Congress were elected to fill their husbands' terms—for the sheer size of you. Lobbyists whisper in the halls: "She looks like she might be God, if God turns out to be a black woman." Your private office is far from the House floor, so you set up a makeshift office right there in one of the rows of seats, just off the center aisle, in the eyeline of the presiding officer. You are here to get things done, to use your voice, which is eloquent and strong. As the chairwoman of the Commission on Immigration Reform, you are a staunch defender of birthright citizenship. "I felt somehow for many years that George Washington and Alexander Hamilton just left me out by mistake," you say. "But through the process of amendment, interpretation, and court decision I have finally been included in 'We, the people.'" You carry a copy of the Constitution in your purse.

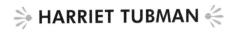 HARRIET TUBMAN

MATRON SAINT OF FREEDOM
B. APPROX. 1822, UNITED STATES
Feast Day: March 10

Much and little is known about the woman whose image may yet displace President Andrew Jackson's on the twenty-dollar bill. She is an American icon of near-mythical proportions, though we cannot say for certain what year she was born. Her name has become inextricably bound to the Underground Railroad and the slaves she smuggled to freedom. (A former slave herself, she became known as "the Moses of her people.") She is less widely recognized for her contributions to the Union Army during the Civil War. In June 1863—she would have been around forty—Tubman became the first woman to lead an armed assault during that war. The Combahee River Raid, led by Tubman and Union Colonel James Montgomery, and remembered by *The New York Times* as "arguably the most beautiful scene ever recorded in a war," facilitated the escape of more than seven hundred men, women, and children—the largest liberation of slaves in American history. Tubman, who lived until 1913, is even less well-known for her contributions late in her life to the cause of women's rights; she became, according to one biographer, "a grand old lady on the suffrage circuit." When asked, sometime after the Civil War, if she believed women should have the right to vote, Tubman answered, "I suffered enough to believe it."

 HYPATIA OF ALEXANDRIA

MATRON SAINT OF SCHOLARS
B. 355 C.E., EGYPT
Feast Day: March 14

Mme. Swann, majestic, smiling, kind, as she advanced along the Avenue du Bois, saw like Hypatia, beneath the slow tread of her feet, worlds revolving.

—MARCEL PROUST, translated by C. K. Scott Moncrieff

The life of the mathematician and philosopher Hypatia is so beset with mystery that we run the risk of pretending to know everything, filling in the blanks as it suits us. Her writing does not survive, though we can say with certainty that she lectured in advanced geometry and astronomy (including how to design an astrolabe, an astronomical calculator that would be used until the nineteenth century). As a philosopher, she belonged to the Neoplatonic school and held great influence in Alexandria among the pagan intellectual elite. But it is her death, rather than her life, that is best known to us. Cyril, the Christian patriarch of Alexandria, demanded the expulsion of the city's Jews, and Hypatia was one of the most prominent members of his opposition. After a day of lectures at the university, she was abducted by a mob of Christian monks, stripped, and beaten in a church, her skin flayed with broken bits of pottery; then her body was dragged outside the city walls and burned. The university and the pagan temples were destroyed soon after. An 1853 novelization of the event by English writer Charles Kingsley drives home how much we want Hypatia to be an ideal heroine; Kingsley depicts Hypatia as she "rose for one moment to her full height, naked, snow-white against the dusky mass around—shame and indignation in those wide clear eyes, but not a stain of fear": the height of martyrdom. But Hypatia's contribution to history came from more than just her death. As noted by one historian, Hypatia's murder "marked the downfall of Alexandrian intellectual life." (Cyril was eventually made a saint.)

 YAYOI KUSAMA

MATRON SAINT OF VISIONARIES
B. 1929, JAPAN
Feast Day: March 22

The visions started in childhood—flowers would talk to her; the floor would disappear. It didn't help that her mother was abusive, her father absorbed in love affairs. Nor that she was sent, at thirteen, to work in a military factory during World War II. Her art became a way of managing her visions, making them concrete. "I would cover a canvas with nets, then continue painting them on the table, on the floor and finally on my own body.... I forgot about myself as they enveloped me." The experience is echoed in her wildly popular *Obliteration Room*, in which visitors enter a white chamber and are invited to cover its surfaces with different-colored polka-dot stickers. In our age of social media, Instagrammers respond emphatically to the psychedelic, seemingly joyful tone of Kusama's immersive environments. During the first week of her retrospective at the Hirshhorn Museum, in Washington, D.C., a visitor tripped and shattered a sculpture while trying to take a selfie. Around the same time, *The Washington Post* reported, "The Kusama selfie is becoming a visual cliché." But these posts miss the art's dark undercurrent. Though Kusama is one of our wealthiest contemporary female artists, she has lived voluntarily at a mental hospital in Tokyo since the 1970s. "By translating hallucinations and fear of hallucinations into paintings, I have been trying to cure my disease," she says. Now, in her eighties, she still refers to herself as "aspiring": "When I was a kid, I had a hard time convincing my mother that I wanted to become an artist. Is it really true that I am famous and successful?"

EMMY NOETHER

MATRON SAINT OF SYMMETRY
B. 1882, GERMANY
Feast Day: March 23

Despite her clear mathematical talent, Emmy Noether was not allowed to enroll as a student at the University of Erlangen, in Germany; the school's Academic Senate ruled that mixed-sex classes would "overthrow all academic order." Instead, Noether audited classes, getting special permission from professors until she was able to obtain her PhD. Her expertise grew from there. Noether's most famous theorem, published in 1918, brilliantly proved that the laws of physics remain the same regardless of when they are applied—the total energy of the universe will be conserved regardless. A ball thrown in the air today will behave the same way if it is thrown tomorrow. For every differentiable symmetry, there is a corresponding conservation law. Although her theorem addressed a central problem in Albert Einstein's general theory of relativity, she faced the same discrimination from universities when seeking employment as she had as an aspiring student. One faculty member protested, "What will our soldiers think when they return to the university and find they are required to learn at the feet of a woman?" Things grew more difficult when, as a Jew, she was forced to flee Germany in 1933. Only late in her life, with help from Albert Einstein, did she make it onto a faculty—at Bryn Mawr, a women's college in Pennsylvania. According to a recent poll conducted at Drexel University, very few students have even heard of Noether, and those who know her name find it difficult to recall what exactly it was that she did—an underwhelming legacy for the woman whom Einstein described as "the most significant creative mathematical genius thus far produced since the higher education of women began."

GLORIA STEINEM

"There was one postcard I used to keep on my wall at *Ms.* It was like poetry; it had everything in it. It said, 'Now that I have read your magazine, I know for sure that you are a commie, lesbian, long-haired dyke, witch, slut, who dates negroids.' And then the finish: 'Isn't that just like a Jew.' They assumed I was Jewish, because they thought feminism was a Jewish plot to divide the Christian family."

In fact, Gloria Steinem's father *was* Jewish; her paternal grand-mother, Pauline, helped get many Jews out of Germany in the 1930s; she was also a vocal member of the National Woman Suffrage Association. Activism, then, was in Steinem's blood, though she says she didn't become an "active feminist" until her thirties, when, in 1969, she went to cover an abortion speakout for *New York* magazine. "There was something," she remarked, "about seeing women tell the truth about their lives in public, and seeing women take seriously something that only happens to women. In my experience, things were only taken seriously if they also happened to men. It made some sense of my own experience—I had had an abortion and had never told anyone. It was one of those moments when you ask, 'Why? Who said?'" Three years later, *Ms.* magazine, Steinem's brain-child, released its first issue. Across two pages, in big bold letters, ran the words "We have had abortions." It was signed by fifty-three women who had had abortions or supported those who had—among them Billie Jean King, Anaïs Nin, Grace Paley, Susan Sontag, and the *Ms.* founder herself.

SANDRA DAY O'CONNOR

MATRON SAINT OF JUSTICE
B. 1930, UNITED STATES
Feast Day: March 26

To the Editor:

I noticed the following paragraph in the "Topics" section of the Sept. 29 editorial page:

"Is no Washington name exempt from shorthand? One, maybe. The Chief Magistrate responsible for executing the laws is sometimes called the POTUS. The nine men who interpret them are often the SCOTUS. The people who enact them are still, for better or worse, Congress."

According to the information available to me, and which I had assumed was generally available, for over two years now SCOTUS has not consisted of nine men. If you have any contradictory information, I would be grateful if you would forward it as I am sure the POTUS, the SCOTUS and the undersigned (the FWOTSC) would be most interested in seeing it.

This letter appeared in *The New York Times* in October 1983. The so-called FWOTSC—First Woman of the Supreme Court—was Justice Sandra Day O'Connor, appointed in 1981. The upward trajectory of O'Connor's career was remarkable. After graduating from Stanford Law, she found that no firms would interview her. "They said, 'We don't hire women,' and that was a shock to me," she recalled. She reported being just as shocked by the news of her Supreme Court nomination, nearly thirty years later. O'Connor went on to be an unpredictable justice—a conservative who upheld *Roe v. Wade*. The difficulty she'd experienced as a woman early on ensured that she would not forget the importance of her role. (So, too, did the absence of a women's restroom anywhere near the court.) "It became very important that I perform in a way that wouldn't provide some reason or cause not to have more women in the future."

WANGARI MAATHAI

She explained it like this: Imagine a country as a stool with three legs. One leg represents democracy, a good government that respects mankind. Another represents peace. The final leg represents accountability, regard for our natural resources. Without those three legs, the base becomes unstable; the stool falls apart. The problem, she said, is that the stool is too often built on only two legs—the third is forgotten. "We don't have a broad sense of accountability and equal distribution of resources. The desire to consume... seems to outpace the sense of responsibility for our resource-intensive lifestyles."

Wangari Maathai devoted her life to trying to correct this imbalance. She began in her home country of Kenya, where she observed women in the countryside struggling every day for basic needs—water, food, an income. "I realized that there are very serious activities such as deforestation, loss of the soil that was gradually destroying that environment and impoverishing them," she recalled. And so she began planting trees. With the grassroots organization she founded in 1977, the Green Belt Movement, she planted fifty million of them. In the process, GBM trained thirty thousand women in forestry and food processing, allowing them to earn their own income. In 2004, seven years before she died, Maathai received the Nobel Peace Prize for her efforts, becoming the first African woman to do so. "For thirty years I worked putting one foot in front of the other and really didn't think anybody was listening to me.... And then suddenly, the Norwegian Nobel Peace Committee tells me that 'You're the one that has been looking at the right balance,'" she said. "We need to continue that message even more strongly, and even with greater conviction until we win. Because we are the ones who are on the right path."

MAYA ANGELOU

"In times of strife and extreme stress, I was likely to retreat to mutism. Mutism is so addictive. And I don't think its powers ever go away." A surprising admission for a woman who, by age forty, had lived in Egypt, in Ghana, and all around the United States; who'd worked as a professional dancer, a prostitute, an activist, a singer, a lecturer; and who would become a prolific writer.

Severe childhood trauma triggered Maya Angelou's mutism at the age of eight: she'd been raped, and after her testimony in court, her rapist had been violently murdered. Her muteness lasted for nearly five years before lifting—but its dark appeal never left her. "It's always there saying, 'You can always come back to me. You have nothing to do—just stop talking.'" Angelou resisted the urge. At forty-one, she published her first and best-known book, *I Know Why the Caged Bird Sings*, which tells the story of that early trauma. In plays, in poems, in autobiographies and spoken-word albums and children's books, she would tell stories for the rest of her life. "The writer has to take the most used, most familiar objects—nouns, pronouns, verbs, adverbs—ball them together and make them bounce, turn them a certain way and make people get into a romantic mood; and another way, into a bellicose mood," she said at age seventy-five. "I'm most happy to be a writer."

KITTY CONE

MATRON SAINT OF ALL BODIES
B. 1944, UNITED STATES
Feast Day: April 7

Kitty Cone went the first fifteen years of her life not knowing what was wrong with her body. Getting around was difficult; one school-teacher observed that she walked on her toes. A military brat, Cone was entitled to free treatment at army hospitals, but the care she received there was often poor. "It's like an HMO only it's worse," she later joked. "They didn't know what my disability was." She endured several misdiagnoses and painful surgeries before a doctor spoke the words "muscular dystrophy," but putting a name to her disease did not lower the barriers she faced or stop the discrimination that confronted a woman in a wheelchair. Later in her life, another doctor persuaded her to get sterilized, waiving the customary waiting period most able-bodied women had to undergo before they could have such a procedure. "Clearly there was such a double standard and I was meant to be sterilized," she said. In 1977, Cone went to San Francisco to help organize a twenty-eight-day sit-in at a federal building, sleeping on the floor in a closet off a conference room. "I had to be turned over at night," she recalled. "I remember I was wolfing down sleeping pills to get through the pain." That sit-in led to the implementation of Section 504 of the Rehabilitation Act, the first U.S. disability civil rights law. Cone stayed in the Bay Area, work-ing at the Berkeley Center for Independent Living, where she cru-saded for handicap-accessible public transportation and curb ramps. When adoption agencies in the United States found her incapable of raising a child, she went to Tijuana, Mexico, to adopt a son. Cone was fifteen when the doctor who identified her muscular dystrophy predicted that she wouldn't live to see age twenty. She died on March 21, 2015; she was seventy. "Oh, I loved what I did with my life," she said.

DOLORES HUERTA

MATRON SAINT OF WORKERS
B. 1930, UNITED STATES
Feast Day: April 10

Divorced, with three children, Alicia Chávez Fernández held two jobs to keep the family afloat, spending her days as a waitress and her nights working at a cannery. When she married her second husband, Alicia was able to acquire a seventy-room hotel in Stockton, California. It was there that her daughter, Dolores, grew up. The hotel was in a working-class neighborhood, and Dolores's mother welcomed low-wage workers, reducing or waiving their fees altogether. This was not the only lesson Huerta learned. "My mother was, of course, very supportive of me as a young woman," she recalled, "and always pushed me to be out in front, to speak my mind, to get involved, to be active." Huerta's activism first came to national attention in the 1960s, when, alongside Cesar Chavez, she co-founded the labor union United Farm Workers and led the Delano grape strike, a five-year labor action against California grape growers, uniting Filipino and Mexican workers. The strike was a success: grape growers signed their first union contracts, benefiting thousands of the nation's lowest paid workers. Huerta also coined UFW's motto, *Sí, se puede* ("*Yes, one can*")—the English translation of which inspired President Barack Obama's 2008 campaign slogan. "Dolores was very gracious when I told her I had stolen her slogan," Obama joked in 2012, when he awarded her the Presidential Medal of Freedom. "Knowing her, I'm glad she let me off easy, because Dolores does not play."

RACHEL CARSON

At a Kaiser Foundation symposium in San Francisco, in October 1963, Rachel Carson stood before an audience of fifteen hundred people and delivered a speech entitled "The Pollution of Our Environment." It had been a whirlwind year since the publication of her book *Silent Spring*, which had prompted President Kennedy to establish a committee to investigate pesticides, effectively launching the modern environmental movement.

The year had been a whirlwind for other reasons as well. Carson had been showered with invitations to speak since the release of *Silent Spring*, but she could accept few of them. The pain was too great. The cancer had metastasized, and her body had burns from the radiation. Even the wig she wore when she went out was hot and itchy. And no one—her critics in particular—could know of her condition, for fear it might be used to call her objectivity into question: *Silent Spring*'s unprecedented claim was that petrochemicals were linked to human cancer. That day in San Francisco, she emphasized the urgency of her findings. "We behave, not like people guided by scientific knowledge, but more like the proverbial bad housekeeper who sweeps dirt under the rug in the hope of getting it out of sight." "The Pollution of Our Environment" would be her last speech; she died six months later. But that day Carson's eyes were set on a life beyond the limits of her own: "The threat is infinitely greater to the generations unborn; to those who have no voice in the decisions of today, and that fact alone makes our responsibility a heavy one."

THE BRONTË SISTERS

MATRON SAINTS OF DREAMERS
B. 1816, 1818, AND 1820, ENGLAND
Feast Day: April 15

The three sisters grew up motherless and poor. Their brother, Branwell, was expected to be the genius of the family, so the girls spent their afternoons reading and writing stories for one another, putting on plays for which they would be the only audience. They wrote their manuscripts in a hand so tiny that no adult had the eyesight to read them. (One of young Charlotte's miniature books was more than sixty thousand words long.) Eventually, though, they had to leave their enclosed world to take work teaching and governessing, jobs they found hateful. Charlotte wrote, "A private governess has no existence, is not considered as a living and rational being except as connected with the wearisome duties she has to fulfill." As a teacher, Emily told her students that she preferred the school dog to any of them. Anne left her post as a governess when her errant brother, who'd been brought on as a tutor, began an ill-fated affair with the lady of the house. (Anne wrote of the incident that she was "sick of mankind and their disgusting ways.") The sisters may have detested the work, but it made for great material. From her experience, Anne produced *Agnes Grey*, a novel whose governess heroine yearns to "go out into the world; to act for myself." Charlotte's *Jane Eyre* also featured a governess as its heroine, while the narrator of Emily's classic *Wuthering Heights* is a servant. When *Agnes Grey*, *Jane Eyre*, and *Wuthering Heights* were published—all in the same year, 1847—all three initially appeared under male pseudonyms. Soon after Charlotte revealed their identities to a stunned publisher, she regretted the confession; the sisters' private world of invention was private no more. "What author," she later wrote, "would be without the advantage of being able to walk invisible?"

⇒ NINA SIMONE ⇐

MATRON SAINT OF SOUL
B. 1933, UNITED STATES
Feast Day: April 21

The name of this tune is "Mississippi Goddam"
And I mean every word of it

—NINA SIMONE

On a Sunday morning in September 1963, dynamite was detonated in the Sixteenth Street Baptist Church in Birmingham, Alabama. The bomb, planted by white supremacists, was timed to go off during Sunday school classes; four little girls were killed. It was a pivotal moment for the growing civil rights movement in the United States, as well as for one of its most vocal proponents. Born Eunice Waymon, the daughter of a North Carolina preacher, she'd wanted to be a concert pianist. Her music then didn't even have words. But as she became Nina Simone, the "high priestess of soul," the words found her. "When I heard about the bombing of the church in which the four little black girls were killed in Alabama," she said, "I shut myself up in a room and that song happened." The result was "Mississippi Goddam," a rallying cry for the movement, and one of Simone's most famous protest songs.

Everybody knows about Mississippi—goddam.

 ERMA BOMBECK

MATRON SAINT OF WOMEN IN THE HOME
B. 1927, UNITED STATES
Feast Day: April 22

"Every morning, we see the men driving out of paradise onto the freeway and into the city. Leaving us to what?" Erma Bombeck wrote in her book *The Grass Is Always Greener over the Septic Tank*. Bombeck was a humorist, but this was from a section called "Loneliness." It begins, "No one talked about it a lot, but everyone knew what it was. It was the day you alphabetized your spices on the spice rack." Bombeck discussed depression as a condition that "came with the territory." The territory was the home, the confines of the housewife, which Bombeck knew about firsthand. Her column "At Wit's End" was nationally syndicated, read by women across the country who could not name the particular problem that plagued them. Bombeck reached them by making them laugh. Her appeal was so broad and her approach so disarming that she lost many conservative fans when, in 1978, she came out swinging in favor of the Equal Rights Amendment. Even when Bombeck was writing about what changes she might make to her life were she to live it over again, she offset the light with the dark. "There would have been more I love yous, more I'm sorrys, more I'm listenings.... Given another shot at life, I would seize every minute of it." But also: "I would never have insisted the car windows be rolled up on a summer day because my hair had just been teased and sprayed."

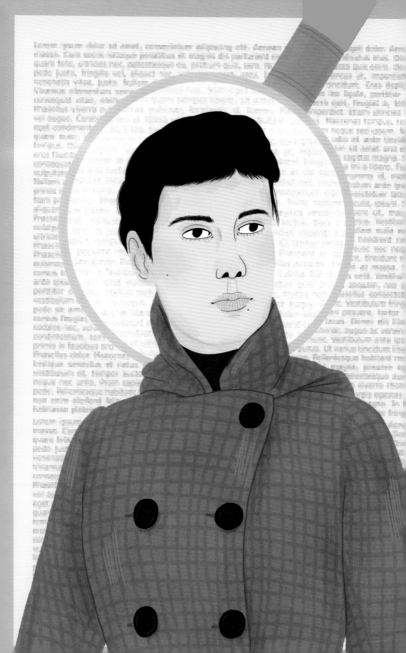

NELLIE BLY

MATRON SAINT OF JOURNALISTS
B. 1864, UNITED STATES
Feast Day: May 5

One was committed by her husband, to correct a fondness for other men. Another was told that this was where all the poor who'd applied for aid were sent. Sixteen hundred women were held captive in Blackwell's Island Insane Asylum—"crippled, blind, old, young, homely, and pretty; one senseless mass of humanity"—and twenty-three-year-old undercover journalist Nellie Bly was determined to document it. Bly is best remembered for her seventy-two-day trip around the world, a real-life enactment of Jules Verne's adventure novel *Around the World in Eighty Days*, but her undercover piece "Ten Days in a Madhouse" was her first great contribution to journalism. Once her put-on antics succeeded in getting her committed, Bly was stripped and made to bathe in ice water alongside other patients, then sent to sleep, freezing, without a nightgown. The days were long, the nights full of screams. The food was foul—old bread and cold tea—and patients were punished if they failed to finish their allotments. Punishment was common, and harsh. Women were beaten, or locked in closets. The experience was enough to drive any person mad. "As I passed a low pavilion, where a crowd of helpless lunatics were confined, I read a motto on the wall, 'While I live I hope,'" Bly wrote in her account. "The absurdity of it struck me forcibly. I would have liked to put above the gates that open to the asylum, 'He who enters here leaveth hope behind.'" But Bly brought about some hope herself: her piece about her experience led to a grand jury investigation, a significantly increased budget for the Department of Public Charities and Corrections, and a new standard in investigative journalism.

PHILLIS WHEATLEY

MATRON SAINT OF READERS
B. 1753, WEST AFRICA
Feast Day: May 8

The first black American to publish a volume of poems, and the second American woman to do so, was called Phillis Wheatley—a name given to her not by her parents but by her owners. The Wheatleys of Boston named her after the slave ship that carried her from West Africa. She was seven. The Wheatley family, known progressives, encouraged young Phillis's education. "Without any Assistance from School Education, and by only what she was taught in the Family," John Wheatley wrote, "she, in sixteen Months Time from her Arrival, attained the English Language, to which she was an utter Stranger before, to such a Degree, as to read any, the most difficult Parts of the Sacred Writings, to the great Astonishment of all who heard her." Many colonists doubted the authenticity of Phillis's talents, and to silence skeptics, she endured an examination in court. When her collection, *Poems on Various Subjects, Religious and Moral,* was published in 1773, she became the most famous African on the planet—according to Henry Louis Gates, Jr., "the Oprah Winfrey of her time." Eventually gaining her freedom, she became a voice for the colonists as the American Revolution approached, writing such poems as "To His Excellency General Washington." In 1776, Washington received her at his headquarters in Cambridge. Despite all her success and apparent patriotism, however, Wheatley recognized the complexity of her position, and her writing foreshadowed another great war, still nearly a century away. From her poem "On Being Brought from Africa to America":

> Some view our sable race with scornful eye,
> "Their colour is a diabolic die."
> Remember, Christians, Negros, black as Cain,
> May be refin'd and join th' angelic train.

 KATHARINE HEPBURN

MATRON SAINT OF LEADING LADIES
B. 1907, UNITED STATES
Feast Day: May 12

In 1931, an ambitious theater collective was founded in New York City by such visionaries as Lee Strasberg and Stella Adler. It was called the Group Theatre, and Katharine Hepburn was *not* among its ranks. She recalled attending one of the group's open sessions: "I thought, as I listened, They're all going to be rather invisible. I told them all I was going to be a great big star—and I left." Hepburn's early confidence was surprising (considering that she was fired as a young actress on several occasions), but it was that assertiveness that would become a signature trait, setting her apart from Hollywood's ingénues. Hepburn played professional women, hardworking lawyers and hardworking athletes and hardworking reporters. Hepburn also played tomboy Jo in the film adaptation of Louisa May Alcott's *Little Women*, and she worked closely with the director Dorothy Arzner, who shared her preference for menswear. (Rumor has it that when RKO Pictures objected to her tailored pants, Hepburn walked around the studio in her underwear.) Hepburn had an extraordinarily long career, in part because she didn't shy from new challenges. "As one goes through life," she wrote in her memoirs, "one learns that if you don't paddle your own canoe, you don't move." At the age of sixty-two, she starred in her first (and only) Broadway musical, about Coco Chanel; she later admitted, "I honestly don't remember ever sitting through a Broadway musical. I certainly never thought I could sing my way through one." She was nominated for a Tony.

BEA ARTHUR

She is known by many as Maude, for her role in the eponymous seventies sitcom, a spin-off of *All in the Family*. Others remember her as Dorothy Zbornak, from *The Golden Girls*. And she is listed as Arthur, Beatrice; Arthur, Bea; and Arthur, Bernice—as well as by her maiden name, Bernice Frankel, and that of her first husband, Robert Alan Aurthur—in the Marine Corps branch of service at the National Archives in St. Louis. A member of the Women's Reserve during World War II, she was stationed in Washington, D.C., as a truck driver and typist. By the time she was honorably discharged, in September 1945, she was a staff sergeant. Her marine qualification card listed her as skilled with a .22-caliber rifle as well as with a bow and arrow. Later in her life, she became an advocate for LGBT rights and an animal rights activist (she was the late honorary director of PETA; a dog park near its headquarters in Virginia is named in her honor). With her two best-known characters, Arthur helped create new roles for strong, commanding women. "Look," she said in one interview, "I'm five feet nine, I have a deep voice and I have a way with a line. What can I do about it? I can't stay home waiting for something different."

FRANCES PERKINS

MATRON SAINT OF CIVIL SERVANTS
B. 1880, UNITED STATES
Feast Day: May 14

Q: What American woman had the worst childbirth experience?
A: Frances Perkins. She spent twelve years in labor.

This is a joke the tour guides sometimes tell around Washington, D.C. Though there is some irony in the joke—Perkins acknowledged cultivating a matronly appearance to gain the trust of her male peers—it is underwhelming recognition for the fourth secretary of labor in U.S. history and the first woman to hold a cabinet position, thereby securing a place in the presidential line of succession. Perkins credited the Triangle Shirtwaist Factory fire of 1911 with galvanizing her into political action. On a street corner in Greenwich Village, she and so many others witnessed the factory fire that killed 146 garment workers, whose employers kept the stairwells and exits locked; many jumped to their death. The tragedy struck Perkins as part of an "ongoing assault on common order." In response, she began working in New York State government, rising to the rank of commissioner of the state's Department of Labor. In 1933, she accepted the position of secretary of labor from President Franklin Delano Roosevelt, with some stipulations: she wanted a minimum wage, a forty-hour workweek, unemployment relief, and the banning of child labor. And she got them. Among all her achievements, Perkins would later say that her greatest was the Social Security Act. Giving a speech at Social Security Administration headquarters, at the age of eighty-two, she stated, "One thing I know: Social Security is so firmly embedded in the American psychology today that no politician . . . could possibly destroy this Act and still maintain our democratic system. It is safe. It is safe forever, and for the everlasting benefit of the people of the United States."

AMELIA EARHART

MATRON SAINT OF TAKING FLIGHT
B. 1897, UNITED STATES
Feast Day: May 20

In June 1928, Amelia Earhart became the first woman to make a transatlantic flight. Though she was celebrated for the journey, she did not fly the plane; it was captained by two male pilots. "It was a grand experience but all I did was lie on my tummy and take pictures of the clouds," she said upon landing. "I was just baggage, like a sack of potatoes." She added, finding a brighter note, "Maybe someday I'll try it alone." She must have already known she would—she made the trip just four years later, five years after Charles Lindbergh's famous flight. The papers took to calling her "Lady Lindy," but Earhart was no iteration of someone else. As a girl, she climbed trees and shot rats with a rifle, and she kept a scrapbook of magazine and newspaper clippings that mentioned successful women in traditionally male lines of work. Her ambitions were at first broad, but they were always high. Uprooted frequently because of her father's unstable career, she attended six high schools in four years, was said to read four times the required course load, and was ultimately commemorated in her high school yearbook as "the girl in brown who walks alone." (She graduated but skipped the ceremony.) Her ambition finally found its focus at a Toronto flying exhibition when a stunt pilot, having a little fun, swooped down toward her, dangerously close. Earhart stood her ground. "Common sense told me that if something went wrong...the airplane and I would be rolled up in a ball together." Still, she stayed: "I believe that little red airplane said something to me as it swished by." Whatever that was, the words stayed with her all her life.

 MARY CASSATT

MATRON SAINT OF THE FEMININE
B. 1844, UNITED STATES
Feast Day: May 22

How rare to find a Mother's Day card that is as nurturing as the mother it's meant to honor. This UNICEF card ($5), with its etching by Mary Cassatt, is just that.

—*New York* magazine, May 1985

Women and children and women with children: these were painter Mary Cassatt's signature subjects, though the artist never became a mother herself. Cassatt, like her close friend Edgar Degas, never married, devoting herself to her art. For a woman, this was a difficult road—of her chosen career, her father reportedly told her, "I'd rather see you dead first." But Cassatt relied on no man, and her subjects, though decidedly feminine, are just as decidedly feminist. Her women appear in quiet moments, peering through binoculars at the opera, reading a newspaper in the garden, bathing a child at home. In 1892, she accepted a commission for the following year's Chicago World's Fair, a large mural meant to depict the advancement of women through history. Degas, who liked to compliment her by saying, "No woman has the right to draw like that," inadvertently encouraged her to take on the project. "As the bare idea of such a thing put Degas into a rage," she wrote, "I got my spirit up and said I would not give up the idea for anything." The final work, *Modern Woman*, which has not survived, was a triptych; the largest panel (*Young Women Plucking the Fruits of Knowledge or Science*) featured a sort of Garden of Eden idyll, overrun with women and no men. "An American friend asked me in rather a huffy tone the other day, 'Then this is woman apart from her relations to man?!'" she wrote. "I told him it was. Men I have no doubt are painted in all their vigor on the walls of other buildings."

SIMONE DE BEAUVOIR

MATRON SAINT OF PHILOSOPHERS
B. 1908, FRANCE
Feast Day: May 24

When Betty Friedan went to visit Simone de Beauvoir in Paris, she felt "the thrill of meeting a cultural hero in person." But though de Beauvoir's work had been a great influence on Friedan, the women failed to see eye to eye. "As soon as a girl is born," de Beauvoir told Friedan, "she is given the vocation of motherhood because society really wants her washing dishes.... If she is conditioned from birth to think that she *should* have children, when she is twenty she no longer has a choice." Friedan replied, "You were the only woman in an intellectual circle. Now society is a little different." She went on: "Is it possible that in your generation...it seemed necessary to make a choice between one thing or the other?" De Beauvoir acquiesced: "I thought I couldn't have children because I wanted to write. But we are getting away from the subject."

Modern readers of *The Second Sex* might balk, as Friedan did, at some of de Beauvoir's extremism—she compares the fetus to "a parasite" and describes conjugal love as a mixture of "attachment, resentment, hatred, rules, resignation, laziness and hypocrisy." But to Friedan it was "no matter": "She started me out on a road on which I'll keep moving." As Judith Thurman wrote in her introduction to a new translation: "To a young feminist perhaps, for whom the very title may seem as quaint as a pair of bloomers—I would suggest that the best way to appreciate *The Second Sex* is to read it in the spirit it was written: as a deep and urgent personal meditation on a true hope that, as she will probably discover, is still elusive for many of us: to become, in every sense, one's own woman."

DOROTHEA LANGE

MATRON SAINT OF THE SELF-TAUGHT
B. 1895, UNITED STATES
Feast Day: May 26

A childhood bout with polio left her with a damaged right leg and a limp that, she said, "formed me, guided me, instructed me, helped me and humiliated me." Her mother encouraged her to become a schoolteacher, saying it would be something to "fall back on." "That, I think, is a detestable phrase for a young person," Lange later remarked. Instead she decided to be a photographer, though she'd never owned a camera—that part didn't seem to matter; the skills would come later. She got her education on the job, taking photographs for the federal Farm Security Administration, documenting rural poverty, migrant workers, displaced farmers. "We found our way in, slid in on the edges. We used our hunches," she recalled. She learned that most people wanted to be looked at. "Who pays attention to you, really, a hundred percent? Your doctor, your dentist, and your photographer." In 1964, a year before her death, Lange was hoping to put together a new project, similar to the one she did for the FSA, documenting poverty in America. "If you encounter anyone who is an extraordinary pictureman, let me know," she said at the end of one interview. "I'll do what I can," the interviewer replied. "And I want to thank you—" "It doesn't have to be a photographer," she interrupted to add.

ISADORA DUNCAN

MATRON SAINT OF MOVEMENT
B. 1877, UNITED STATES
Feast Day: May 27

"Art was whatever Isadora did," wrote John Dos Passos in his trilogy, *U.S.A.* Edith Wharton remarked that the first time she saw Duncan dance, "it shed a light on every kind of beauty." It is hard to know what Duncan's dancing was like—she would allow no one to film her performances—though perhaps no footage would have been able to do justice to her presence. "She had the most extraordinary quality of repose," recalled the choreographer Frederick Ashton. "She would stand for what seemed quite a long time doing nothing, and then make a very small gesture that seemed full of meaning." Ashton was only seventeen when he saw Duncan perform at a theater in London in 1921. By then Duncan was in her forties, fat and drunk and perpetually broke. She was living on the other side of tragedy: it had been eight hard years since the car carrying her two young children slid into the Seine, drowning them both. This loss was the greatest sorrow in a life beset with great sorrows as well as great triumphs. Her father died in a shipwreck; she claimed to have developed her untamed method of dance while watching waves break along the shore. She even managed to die notoriously, when her scarf caught the rear wheel of the automobile in which she was riding. Duncan danced with the same madness, the same freedom with which she lived. As she put it: "From the first I have only danced my life."

⤜ SOJOURNER TRUTH ⤛

MATRON SAINT OF ORATORS
B.1797, UNITED STATES
Feast Day: June 1

Man is so selfish that he has got women's rights and his own too.

—SOJOURNER TRUTH

There exists no faithful transcript of Sojourner Truth's most famous speech, delivered at the Women's Rights Convention in Akron, Ohio, in 1851 and referred to by its refrain, "Ain't I a Woman?" Truth spoke off the cuff (she could not read or write); in Ohio's *Anti-Slavery Bugle*, it was reported as "one of the most unique and interesting speeches" at the convention. "It is impossible," the report said, to "convey any adequate idea of the effect it produced upon the audience. Those only can appreciate it who saw her powerful form, her whole-souled, earnest gestures, and listened to her strong and truthful tones." In later retellings, her speech would be presented in southern dialect, when in fact Truth spoke with a Dutch accent, Dutch having been her first language. Though a symbol for emancipated slaves in the South, Truth was from New York. As Isabella Baumfree, she was born into slavery in 1797, near the Hudson River, and as Isabella, she escaped to freedom along with her infant daughter after her owner reneged on his promise to emancipate her. "I did not run off, for I thought that wicked," she later said, "but I walked off, believing that to be all right." Only in 1843, as the historian Carleton Mabee told it, did Isabella emerge, at the age of forty-six, as "a national figure in the movements to advance the rights of women and blacks." "The Lord gave me the name Sojourner," she said, "because I was to travel up and down the land showing the people their sins and being a sign unto them. Afterward I told the Lord I wanted another name because everybody had two names; and the Lord gave me Truth, because I was to declare the truth to the people."

 JOSEPHINE BAKER

MATRON SAINT OF THE INDEPENDENT
B. 1906, UNITED STATES
Feast Day: June 3

In her 1934 film, *Zouzou*—the first major motion picture to star an African American actress—Josephine Baker famously danced partnerless alongside her own shadow, smiling and shimmying in a glittering one-piece. It is a fitting image for a woman who possessed the courage and dynamism of several people. The daughter of a washerwoman, née Freda Josephine McDonald, she got her start dancing on street corners for change. "One day I realized I was living in a country where I was afraid to be black," she later said, and so she sailed to Paris, where she rose to fame at the Folies Bergère. In Europe, she went on to be known as the Black Venus, the Amber Queen, and the Creole Goddess. Pablo Picasso called her "the Nefertiti of now." She became a spy for the French Resistance in the thirties and forties, pinning messages inside her underwear. In the fifties and sixties, she was an activist for the civil rights movement, appearing alongside Martin Luther King, Jr., and Rosa Parks at the March on Washington. There were four husbands, and four divorces. Twelve adopted children from all around the world—her "Rainbow Tribe." Also a slew of exotic pets, including Chiquita, a diamond-collared cheetah from one of her Paris nightclub acts. (In another, she wore a skirt made of rubber bananas.) She adopted her country as well, becoming perhaps the only Frenchwoman to have been born in St. Louis, Missouri. Baker embodied a spirit from which it is still hard to look away. Regarding a clip from *Zouzou* posted on YouTube nearly eighty years later, a commenter wrote, "One of the first people to smile with their whole body."

⇒ THE WILLIAMS SISTERS ⇐

MATRON SAINTS OF ATHLETES
B. 1980 AND 1981, UNITED STATES
Feast Day: June 7

In 2001, at ages twenty and nineteen, Venus and Serena Williams were set to play against each other at the Indian Wells Masters tournament. The day of the match, Venus pulled out of the competition, citing tendinitis. When Serena played a solo match a couple of days later, she received boos from the crowd and reported hearing racial slurs. Serena won, though she spent the next several hours crying in the locker room. "If you can boo a teenager, and you can be white and sixty years old, you know what?" Serena later said in an interview. "I'm *cool* on you."

The Williams sisters had worked their whole lives to get to where they were. At seven and eight years old, they'd begun training under the hot sun on the public courts in Southern California. "Good shot," their father and trainer, Richard Williams, would say. "Thank you, Daddy," the older girl would answer. This was Compton in the late 1980s; the girls would hit the court when they heard gunshots nearby, or so the legend goes. Richard taped promotional posters to telephone poles early in their careers; one read, "Venus Williams Is Straight Outta Compton!" The girls practiced before and after school, chauffeured around in a yellow VW bus along with a grocery cart full of tennis balls. "The girls are going to be professional," their mother and coach, Oracene, remembered thinking. "We're going to need a lawyer, and we're going to need an accountant." Two young African American girls, set to dominate a historically white sport. And they did dominate, taking turns winning a No. 1 ranking from the Women's Tennis Association in singles and sharing that distinction in doubles. After fourteen years of boycotting the tournament, Serena came back to Indian Wells in 2015. Again she won.

 ANNE FRANK

MATRON SAINT OF DIARISTS
B. 1929, GERMANY
Feast Day: June 12

"The two of us looked out at the blue sky, the bare chestnut tree glistening with dew," Anne Frank wrote in February 1944, "and we were so moved and entranced that we couldn't speak." Frank spent the two years she chronicled in her diary—before being arrested and imprisoned in the Bergen-Belson concentration camp, where she died at age fifteen—indoors, longing to be outside. "Our chestnut tree is in leaf," she wrote another day, "and here and there you can already see a few small blossoms." The tree stood just beyond the attic window; she kept time by it, kept by it an idea of some imagined other life. Later: "Our chestnut tree is in full bloom. It's covered with leaves and is even more beautiful than last year." Anne Frank's tree stood for another sixty-five years, until even a steel support structure failed to save it. On June 12, 2017—which would have been Frank's eighty-eighth birthday—a white-flowered horse chestnut tree was planted in her honor at Liberty Park in lower Manhattan. The tree was one of dozens grown from seeds of the original that are planted around the world.

THE MIRABAL SISTERS

MATRON SAINTS OF REBELS
B. 1924, 1926, AND 1935, DOMINICAN REPUBLIC
Feast Day: June 14

To the Dominicans leading the movement against dictator Rafael Trujillo, Minerva, María Teresa, and Patria Mirabal were *Las Mariposas*, or "the Butterflies"—fighters who withstood incarceration to unite the middle class against the dictatorship, martyrs who ultimately lost their lives to Trujillo's henchmen. To Dedé Mirabal, they were her sisters. "Minerva was the brains, Mate the fire, Patria the glue, and me? I am the one who gets to spread their story for generations." While Dedé's husband would not allow her to join her sisters in their fight, the Butterflies led the Movement of the Fourteenth of June, named for the date of one of Trujillo's massacres, meeting in secret, amassing weapons, and distributing information about the victims unjustly killed under Trujillo's regime. The sisters knew what danger they were in. "Perhaps what we have most near is death, but that idea doesn't frighten me," María Teresa said. "We shall continue to fight for that which is just." When news of their murder reached the public—Trujillo had had them beaten and strangled, after which their bodies were loaded into their car, which was pushed off a mountain road—it only served to embolden the rebellion. Trujillo was assassinated six months later. In the 1990s, Dedé founded the Mirabal Sisters Museum and established a foundation in their honor. "It may hurt when I reflect on all that I have lost," she said, "but I beam with pride when I reflect on how much we have gained from them. It is an honor to spread their story."

BENAZIR BHUTTO

MATRON SAINT OF DEMOCRACY
B. 1953, PAKISTAN
Feast Day: June 21

The streets of Karachi, Pakistan, were packed with welcoming crowds. Former prime minister Benazir Bhutto had returned after nine years of self-imposed exile following a military coup by Pervez Musharraf, a former four-star general. Bhutto waved to her supporters from a motorcade. She had come to prepare for Pakistan's 2008 elections as the candidate of the PPP—the left-wing, socialist-progressive Pakistan Peoples Party, which her father, Zulfikar Ali Bhutto, had founded. But something was wrong. The streetlights, she noticed, were going off in sequence. Then came the explosions—two suicide bombs, resulting in 180 deaths and 500 injuries, most of the victims members of the PPP. The attack was believed to have been sponsored by the state, as Musharraf's government had failed to provide even basic security measures. Bhutto, who survived the assassination attempt, went home to her children in Dubai, but for only a few days. Her younger daughter, Aseefa, remembers her saying, "Life is in God's hands. If I die, it's God's choice." Her elder daughter, Bakhtawar, would turn eighteen the following month. The night before Bhutto was to leave again, she wished her daughter a happy birthday. "After she was gone, I found this necklace in her drawer. It said, Happy eighteenth birthday," Bakhtawar recalled. "So I feel like she was prepared." Bhutto returned to Pakistan and to another assassination attempt. This time, she did not survive. Bhutto, whose father and two brothers also gave their lives for their country, believed "that the fight for the truth is important because the day does come when you see the response to your struggle." She did not get to see the response, but Bhutto's assassination set off riots across Pakistan, ultimately bringing the PPP back to power under her message: "Democracy is the greatest revenge."

HELEN KELLER

MATRON SAINT OF OPTIMISM
B. 1880, UNITED STATES
Feast Day: June 27

"If any one would seem to have a right to feel blue, it would be this gifted young lady," begins the *Journal of Education*'s 1903 review of Helen Keller's *Optimism*. It is a favorable review, if not altogether flattering. "One is continually surprised as he reads her words at her fine command of language, at her marvelous acquaintance with history, as well as at the hopefulness of her spirit." *He* may be surprised, but he needn't be. Mark Twain called her "the greatest woman since Joan of Arc," but Keller, who was deaf and blind, is too often spoken of in terms of what she couldn't do, rather than what she did. Her triumph over her disabilities—really the triumph of two women, Keller herself and her teacher and companion, Anne Sullivan—was remarkable: She learned to speak. She even gave speeches. She was an advocate for the disabled, yes. But also a suffragette. And a pacifist. One of the founders of the ACLU. Perhaps it was her difficult beginning that gave her the appetite to affect the world around her. "Knowledge is happiness," she wrote in one of her letters. "To know the thoughts and deeds that have marked man's progress is to feel the great heart-throbs of humanity through centuries; and if one does not feel in these pulsations a heavenward striving, one must indeed be deaf to the harmonies of life." The review of *Optimism* concludes, "[Hers] is the song of a bird; and ears will gladly listen for the rapturous note she sings to them from behind her bars." In truth the bars were long behind her.

FRIDA KAHLO

MATRON SAINT OF COLOR
B. 1907, MEXICO
Feast Day: July 6

A collision on the streets of Mexico City—a wooden bus, an electric trolley car—changed eighteen-year-old Frida Kahlo's life. "First we were in another bus," she recalled, "but I had lost a little umbrella, and we got out to look for it, that's why we got on that bus, which mutilated me." A handrail pierced her lower body, her spinal column and pelvis were broken, and her leg was shattered. Before the accident, she'd wanted to go to medical school; after the accident, she was a patient. It was during her long recovery period that she began to paint seriously, setting up an easel that allowed her to work from bed. Her boyfriend, who'd sustained only minor injuries, found Kahlo in the wreckage that fateful day, and the image he later described sounds plucked from the fantastical paintings she would one day create: "Something strange had happened. Frida was totally nude. The collision had unfastened her clothes. Someone in the bus, probably a house painter, had been carrying a packet of powdered gold. This package broke, and the gold fell all over the bleeding body of Frida. When people saw her, they cried, '*La bailarina, la bailarina!*' With the gold on her red, bloody body, they thought she was a dancer."

MALALA YOUSAFZAI

MATRON SAINT OF STUDENTS
B. 1997, PAKISTAN
Feast Day: July 12

At twelve she kept a diary, documenting life under occupation by a hostile extremist group:

> *The night was filled with artillery fire.*

> *The principal announced vacations but did not mention the date the school was to reopen.... While leaving I looked at the building as if I would not come here again.*

> *I switched on the TV in the evening and heard about the blasts in Lahore. I said to myself, "Why do these blasts keep happening in Pakistan?"*

Subtract the television and the proper nouns, and these entries sound not unlike those from another, more famous diary, one begun in 1942. But while the world had to wait years to read the diary of Anne Frank, this diary, the diary of Malala Yousafzai, was released online nearly as it was written, in 2009, for the BBC Urdu news service. The publication of her writing, along with the *New York Times* documentary about her that followed, gave Malala a platform from which to advocate for female education, a right that was nearly taken from her. The attention also made her a target for the Taliban. At fifteen, she was shot in the head by one of its gunmen—and survived. In her first speech following the attack, she addressed an international Youth Assembly at U.N. headquarters: "Let us pick up our books and pens. They are our most powerful weapons. One child, one teacher, one pen and one book can change the world. Education is the only solution." She received the Nobel Peace Prize a year later, the youngest laureate ever.

GERTRUDE BELL

MATRON SAINT OF TRAVELERS
B. 1868, ENGLAND
Feast Day: July 14

A plaque on the side of a large brick house in North Yorkshire, England, reads, "Gertrude Lowthian Bell at One Time Lived in This House. Scholar, Traveller, Administrator, and Peace Maker. A Friend of the Arabs." Though this was the house where young Gertrude, the daughter of a wealthy industrialist, grew up, it was not the place that felt most like home. Gertrude's uncle was a British minister in Tehran; at twenty-four she went to visit him and the world opened up. Her extensive travels through the Middle East were uncommon for a European, even more so for a Victorian woman, carting along her library, her tent, and her tea set. But she had a strong feeling for the people she met. After World War I, she became a fierce advocate of Arab independence and began working for British intelligence, delivering a report titled "Self-Determination in Mesopotamia." In a 1918 letter from Baghdad, she wrote, "Dearest Father, I am having by far the most interesting time of my life. It doesn't happen often that people are told that their future as a state is in their hands, and asked what they would like." She was the only woman present at the Cairo Conference of 1921, playing a key part in establishing the geographical and political structure of what would be Iraq. She went on to serve on the committee of Iraq's National Library, and founded the Baghdad Archaeological Museum, today known as the National Museum of Iraq. "I have grown to love this land, its sights and its sounds," she wrote to her father. "I never weary of the East, just as I never feel it to be alien.... It is a second native country. If my family were not in England, I should have no wish to return."

ANN AND CECILE RICHARDS

MATRON SAINTS OF MOTHERS AND DAUGHTERS
B. 1933 AND 1957, UNITED STATES
Feast Day: July 15

I had such high expectations of myself. I was going to be the best mother, the best housewife, the best entertainer, the best nurse, you know—what it was, I was going to be the best. And I could never live up to my expectations.   —ANN RICHARDS, former governor of Texas

My mom used to say that as women we keep thinking we're going to be perfect. . . . But it doesn't happen. So she always said to me, If a new opportunity comes, you just have to take it. I think in my day-to-day life I try to channel a little bit of Ann in that.
                —CECILE RICHARDS, president of Planned Parenthood

I did not want my tombstone to read, "She kept a really clean house." I think I'd like them to remember me by saying, "She opened government to everyone."   —ANN

The most discouraging thing we are facing is the thought that our daughters and granddaughters could have fewer rights than we do—Mom never would have stood for it, so I can't either.   —CECILE

I get a lot of cracks about my hair, mostly from men who don't have any.   —ANN

One of my proudest moments as a mother was when Lily, my eldest, was called out by Rush Limbaugh on his radio show, by name. I was like: "My job is done, as a parent."   —CECILE

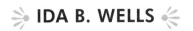 IDA B. WELLS

MATRON SAINT OF RIGHTING WRONGS
B. 1862, UNITED STATES
Feast Day: July 16

A white woman was found dead in Jackson, Tennessee, arsenic in her stomach. A black woman—the white woman's cook—had a box of rat poison at home; it was deemed enough evidence to put her in the county jail. That was where the lynch mob came for her. They hanged her, naked, in the courthouse yard, and shot her body full of bullets. The white woman's husband confessed to poisoning his wife shortly thereafter. In Quincy, Mississippi, a black man suspected of poisoning a well was lynched, too. But the mob, unsure that they'd found the true culprit, cast a wider net: they went on to lynch the man's wife, his mother-in-law, and two friends. "O my God! Can such things be and no justice for it?" wrote Wells. "American Christianity heard of this awful affair and read of its details and neither press nor pulpit gave the matter more than passing comment." Wells's mission was to compel the world to listen. She gave speeches across America and Europe and published investigative pieces, shining a light on how "our country's national crime" had become a way for many white southerners to hinder black economic progress. In 1893, she led a boycott of the Chicago World's Fair (where Mary Cassatt's mural *Modern Woman* was making waves of its own), citing the exposition's exclusion of the black community. "The men who make these charges encourage or lead the mobs which do the lynching. They belong to the race which holds Negro life cheap, which owns the telegraph wires, newspapers, and all other communication with the outside world," she wrote in her pamphlet *The Reason Why the Colored American Is Not in the World's Columbian Exposition.* "Masks have long since been thrown aside and the lynchings of the present day take place in broad daylight." Wells's mission was to make people look.

⋇ SALLY RIDE ⋇

In June 1983, Sally Ride left this planet for six days, two hours, twenty-three minutes, and fifty-nine seconds. She was the first American woman to orbit the Earth, aboard the space shuttle *Challenger*. The days leading up to launch were a media frenzy—NASA was known as a hero factory—but Ride didn't have patience for reporters' more ignorant questions. *Will the flight affect your reproductive organs?* "There's no evidence of that." *Do you weep when things go wrong on the job?* "How come nobody ever asks Rick those questions?" *Will you become a mother?* "You notice I'm not answering." Even articles that pointed out the chauvinistic nature of such questions found time to label Ride "an indifferent housekeeper." Though Ride—a physics PhD who started her career at NASA by answering an advertisement in the Stanford student paper—preferred to be perceived as an astronaut first and a woman second, she devoted her later years to Sally Ride Science, a nonprofit that exposes children to science—with an emphasis on outreach to girls. Thirty-two at the time of the *Challenger* voyage, Ride was also the youngest American astronaut ever to go to space, but it wasn't until the end of her life that she became another kind of hero. In her final days, suffering from pancreatic cancer, Ride decided to come out in her obituary. She became the first known LGBT astronaut. A year later, Ride was posthumously awarded the Presidential Medal of Freedom. Tam O'Shaughnessy, her partner of twenty-seven years, was there to accept it on her behalf.

 BELLA ABZUG

MATRON SAINT OF LAWYERS
B. 1920, UNITED STATES
Feast Day: July 24

The jury deliberated for two and a half minutes. Willie McGee had no chance. He was an African American man accused of raping a white woman in Mississippi, in 1945. This was how it happened for men like McGee in times and places like his. But the unjustness of the trial and the swiftness of the conviction soon garnered attention around the country—a cause célèbre that saw William Faulkner and Albert Einstein speaking out in McGee's defense—and the particular attention of a twenty-eight-year-old lawyer from New York, who took on McGee's appeal. The daughter of Russian Jewish immigrants, Bella Abzug knew prejudice, and she didn't tolerate it. Decades before she was elected to Congress, before her tireless championing of women's lib and gay rights earned her the nickname "Battling Bella," Abzug crafted a defense for McGee founded on a series of civil rights arguments—and, radically, introduced evidence of a consensual interracial affair into the case record. Though the strategy ultimately failed, Abzug succeeded in exposing southern rape law for what it was: a way for those in positions of power to control African Americans while depriving white women of their agency. The assertion that an interracial relationship could be consensual was met with outrage, but Abzug never wavered. The editor of one local newspaper in Jackson declared, "If Mrs. Abzug ever again appears in Mississippi, either as a lawyer or as an individual, it will be one time too often." She traveled to Jackson the very next day.

KASHA NABAGESERA

MATRON SAINT OF COMING OUT
B. 1980, UGANDA
Feast Day: August 1

In October 2010, a weekly tabloid in Uganda called *Rolling Stone* (unaffiliated with the American magazine) ran a front-page piece listing the names and addresses of Uganda's "top 100 homosexuals," accompanied by photographs and a header that read, "Hang Them." Among the one hundred was Kasha Nabagesera, the "founding mother" of the Ugandan LGBT civil rights movement. Nabagesera had a target on her back in Uganda, where homosexuality is illegal, since the age of twenty-three, when she launched Freedom and Roam Uganda (FARUG), a human rights organization aimed at protecting gay and lesbian, bisexual, transgender, and intersex citizens. After that 2010 article, Nabagesera led the charge against the tabloid for violating the constitutional right to privacy of the one hundred people listed, and she won. Though the Ugandan *Rolling Stone* was shut down, many on the list would lose their jobs and their homes, and at least one—activist and "Uganda's first openly gay man," David Kato—lost his life; he was found bludgeoned to death in his home. Despite the threats that are made against her every day, Nabagesera isn't leaving. "Even though my allies cannot be with me, I know there are many. Seeing what activists in other countries are doing, what they have already achieved, keeps us motivated too," she has said. "I may not even live to enjoy what I am fighting for, but I am proud and happy that I have made my contribution for future generations."

MARY EDWARDS WALKER

MATRON SAINT OF SURGEONS
B. 1832, UNITED STATES
Feast Day: August 12

"I don't wear men's clothes, I wear my own clothes," said the first female surgeon in the United States, addressing her proclivity for pants. She found the long skirt that was in fashion at the time, with its layers and layers of petticoats, cumbersome, as well as unhygienic—the multiple hems swept dust and dirt around wherever its wearer went. She wore pants even at her 1855 wedding, where she also refused to include "obey" in her vows and insisted on keeping her own name. After working her way through medical school at Syracuse (the only woman in her class), Mary Edwards Walker found it difficult to maintain a private practice, with so few people willing to choose a female doctor. When the Civil War broke out, the Union Army would only permit her to work as a nurse, and so she practiced, unpaid, as a field surgeon in everything but name until, two years into the war, she was granted the official title. When she was captured by Confederate troops after crossing enemy lines to aid in an amputation, a Confederate captain wrote of being "both amused and disgusted" by the sight of her in full uniform: "not good looking and of course had tongue enough for a regiment of men." She spent four months as a prisoner of war. To this day, she is the only woman to have been awarded a Medal of Honor for her service. Walker spent the remainder of her life working: at a women's prison, then an orphanage, and as an advocate for women's dress reform. She testified twice on women's suffrage before Congress, but she died in 1919, a year before women got the vote. She was buried in a black suit.

JIN XING

MATRON SAINT OF SELF-INVENTION
B. 1967, PEOPLE'S REPUBLIC OF CHINA
Feast Day: August 13

On China's first season of *So You Think You Can Dance*, one judge earned the moniker "Poison Tongue." "Chinese TV always digs at people's scars, consumes their pain. This is the biggest weakness of Chinese TV, and I hate it!" she said, admonishing the host for baiting a contestant into trotting out a sob story. "We won't use people's suffering." Her outburst became a viral sensation; she was given her own show within the year, becoming China's answer to Oprah Winfrey.

Jin Xing is a star of her own making, even a woman of her own making. As a nine-year-old boy, she joined the dance troupe of the People's Liberation Army and quickly climbed the ranks, studying acrobatics, opera, ballet—all while learning to use machine guns. At seventeen, she became the highest-ranked male dancer in the country, winning a dance scholarship that allowed her to study and perform in New York. It was there that she became free to find out who she really was. "That's when I discovered words—'transsexual,' 'transgender.'" It would have been easier to undergo gender-confirmation surgery in America or in Europe—virtually anywhere but her homeland. But, she said, "I wanted to be close to my mom, because the first life she gave me, I was born as Chinese. So the second time I gave myself a birth again, I wanted it to be in China, too." Then, as a transgender, unmarried woman, she adopted three children. (China's one-child policy does not apply to adoption.) Hearing Jin speak in interviews, she seems to be biding her time, preparing for her next great move. "A long time ago, people told me I'd become a politician, and I said, 'I know, but not yet.' All of this, this talk show, everything, it's all preparation."

JULIA CHILD

During World War II, well before she came to be known as Our Lady of the Ladle, Julia McWilliams joined the Office of Strategic Services, a predecessor to the CIA. She was stationed in Kunming, China, where she was assigned to cook up not food but shark repellent, as too many sharks in the area were setting off OSS underwater explosives. While in Kunming, she fell in love, both with her husband—Paul Child—and with food, and when her husband's work with the Foreign Service moved the couple to Paris, she enrolled in the famous culinary school Le Cordon Bleu. The professional culinary world was dominated by men, and her instructors were less than welcoming. Julia found a community by joining a women's cooking club in Paris, Le Cercle des Gourmettes, and started putting together a book. Upon its publication in 1961, *Mastering the Art of French Cooking* was greeted with wild success in the States; it was one of the first cookbooks to present step-by-step directions, making its recipes more accessible to home cooks. When she began hosting *The French Chef* on public television, Julia, six foot two and warbly-voiced, became beloved for making even the preparation of difficult dishes seem within reach; she also knew that her audience "delighted" in her mistakes. A self-proclaimed "natural ham," she kept a large red fire extinguisher in view when something on her stovetop was being flambéed. Dangling an eel one-handed, she told her audience, "You can improve the flavor of your wine by dropping a live eel into the bottle. When you try it, let me know if it works." Her entire kitchen, complete with the custom counters her husband designed to accommodate her height, is on display at the Smithsonian's National Museum of American History, in Washington, D.C., a floor below the original "Star-Spangled Banner" flag.

MADONNA

MATRON SAINT OF POP
B. 1958, UNITED STATES
Feast Day: August 16

There is the "Like a Virgin" Madonna of 1984, in a lace-corseted wedding gown, long white gloves, and a belt buckle that announces BOY TOY, writhing around onstage at the MTV Video Music Awards. There is the "Like a Prayer" Madonna, whose music video—with imagery of burning crosses and a black man being unjustly arrested for a white man's crime—got her condemned by the Vatican. Then there is Madonna the actress, portraying, in *Desperately Seeking Susan*, an extreme precursor to the modern Manic Pixie, airing out her armpits over a public-bathroom hand dryer. Author Madonna arrives in 1992 with *Sex*, a coffee-table book of erotic photographs that generated its own heat, selling 150,000 copies on its first day. Eleven years after that comes *children's book* author Madonna—certainly the only children's book author referred to by *New York* magazine as "S&M's first cultural ambassador." Madonna, who spoke powerfully at the 2017 Women's March in Washington, D.C., has been a force for third-wave feminism for three decades. Here she is, in an interview with MTV in the 1980s, obsessively twirling a blond curl around her finger, big black bows atop her head: "I think you build an image of yourself and the world ends up seeing only that aspect of you. Every person is multifaceted, and hopefully the longer your career goes on, the more you can reveal about yourself. I couldn't tell you what the world doesn't see in me right now—there's a million things."

MAE WEST

MATRON SAINT OF SEX
B. 1893, UNITED STATES
Feast Day: August 17

In 1935, she was the highest-paid woman in the United States and the second-highest-grossing American overall—bested only by William Randolph Hearst, the infamous media tycoon who inspired Orson Welles's *Citizen Kane*. Hearst went after the star for her risqué material in his twenty-eight newspapers, editorializing, "Isn't it time Congress did something about Mae West?" West's battle with censorship was not a new one. Her first big hit, a three-act play called *Sex*, got her arrested for obscenity and briefly jailed. In Hollywood, West made a fortune for Paramount, but her films faced increasing scrutiny under the moral guidelines of the Hays Code, which forbade "any inference of sex perversion." (One song title, "No One Does It Like That Dallas Man," was changed to "No One Loves Me Like That Dallas Man.") West fought the system, going so far as to smuggle uncensored versions of her films into theaters. But perhaps the most shocking thing about West was the broadness of her appeal—to women as well as to men. While the Royal Air Force named an inflatable life vest in her honor, and scientists at Princeton invented the "Mae West magnet," with "curves that raise its power of attraction," West's audiences were made up largely of young women, who gleaned life lessons about independence from her: West's characters enjoyed men; they did not need them. As the great French novelist and West admirer Colette wrote, "She alone, out of an enormous and dull catalogue of heroines, does not get married at the end of the film, does not die, does not take the road to exile, does not gaze sadly at her declining youth in a silver-framed mirror in the worst possible taste."

MARSHA P. JOHNSON

MATRON SAINT OF PROTEST

B. 1945, UNITED STATES

Feast Day: August 24

During the six days of the Stonewall riots in Greenwich Village, protestors threw pennies, formed Rockette-style kick lines in front of the police, and sang "We Shall Overcome." They also smashed windows, knocked down barricades, and faced brutality at the hands of police officers. Marsha P. Johnson, drag queen and gay liberation activist, was spotted front and center on the first night, atop a lamppost, dropping a bag full of bricks onto an empty squad car, shattering its windshield. Johnson was a local celebrity in downtown New York. She wore red plastic high heels, days-old flowers discarded by florists, fake fruit. A salesperson at her local thrift shop remembered her as a "wonderful, sweet person" (also as "the fella that used to buy all the gowns"). She liked to say that her middle initial, P, stood for "Pay It No Mind." The Stonewall riots marked the beginning of a life committed to social activism, aiding trans women and those afflicted with AIDS. When "Mama" Jean DeVente—who would go on to serve as grand marshal of the Christopher Street Liberation Day Parade—was knocked down by an officer and kicked in the face, Johnson used her own blouse to stop the bleeding. "Get up, girl," Johnson told her. "We got a fight on our hands."

 GLADYS ELPHICK

MATRON SAINT OF COMMUNITY
B. 1904, AUSTRALIA
Feast Day: August 27

Gladys Elphick was a young widow when she left the Aboriginal mission at Point Pearce, in 1939. "Point Pearce wasn't a bad place when I was young," she recalled, "but we lived a terribly sheltered life there." Like many Aboriginal Australians, Elphick had been taken to the mission as an infant—part of a government initiative aimed at "assimilation," in which indigenous people were forced onto reserves, and children of mixed descent were removed from their families, now referred to as the Stolen Generations. The Aboriginal Australians Elphick encountered outside of the mission were living in abject poverty. Aboriginal soldiers who'd served in the war were ineligible for the benefits afforded to non-indigenous veterans. A Family Endowment Act payable to mothers excluded the indigenous population. Many Aboriginals worked sixteen-hour days, earning a fraction of what their European counterparts did. "I could hardly believe some of the dreadful things I came across." Elphick joined a variety of activities committees and began to organize, inviting indigenous women in the community to meet in "Aunty Glad's" home; they crowded into her bedroom and took up all the space on the bed. "We wanted to show people, and to show the government, that we could do things for ourselves." She went on to found the Council of Aboriginal Women of South Australia, which led to the establishment of medical and legal services within the community. For her efforts, she was appointed a Member of the Order of the British Empire and was named South Australia's Aborigine of the Year—"[that was] the one I wanted," she later told the Adelaide *Advertiser*, "because it comes from my own people, and that makes it special."

MARY WOLLSTONECRAFT AND MARY SHELLEY

MATRON SAINTS OF CREATION
B. 1759 AND 1797, ENGLAND
Feast Day: August 30

"If I cannot inspire love, I will cause fear; and chiefly towards you my arch-enemy, because my creator, do I swear inextinguishable hatred," the creature tells his creator in Mary Shelley's 1818 gothic classic *Frankenstein*. "You shall curse the hour of your birth." Some literary critics have interpreted the novel as a "birth myth," in which Shelley confronts "the drama of guilt, dread, and flight surrounding birth and its consequences." The subject of childbirth was a fraught one for the author. At eighteen—a year before she would begin writing *Frankenstein*—she suffered the loss of a baby girl, born two months premature. Shelley's own mother, Mary Wollstonecraft, died of childbed fever just eleven days after giving birth to her. Wollstonecraft was an author herself. Her "Thoughts on the Education of Daughters," published in 1787, begins with the assertion that it is "the duty of every rational creature to attend to its offspring." She argued the importance of women's education in "A Vindication of the Rights of Women": "Taught from their infancy that beauty is woman's sceptre, the mind shapes itself to the body, and, roaming round its gilt cage, only seeks to adorn its prison." (She couldn't know the parallel she was making with the creature her daughter would imagine decades later. Much like Frankenstein's monster, women are confined by their own physical form.) Though Wollstonecraft would not live to see the woman her daughter became, she did all she could in her lifetime to ensure that her daughter, and all daughters, would grow up with greater opportunity than the women who came before them.

⋙ MARIA MONTESSORI ⋘

MATRON SAINT OF TEACHERS
B. 1870, ITALY
Feast Day: August 31

Proposed Winter Schedule of Hours in the "Children's Houses" (9A.M.–4P.M.)

9–10. Entrance. Greeting. Inspection as to personal cleanliness.
10–11. Intellectual exercises (nomenclature, sense exercises).

In medical school, Maria Montessori was required to practice on cadavers alone, after hours, as she could not be in the presence of a naked body alongside her male cohorts. Her interests soon turned to pediatrics and psychiatry. Upon graduation, she began working with mentally disabled children.

11–11:30. Simple gymnastics. 11:30–12. Luncheon. Short prayer.

Suspecting that the pedagogy she'd developed with disabled children would also apply to children who weren't disabled, Montessori accepted an offer to work with low-income families in a blue-collar district of Rome. They called it Casa dei Bambini, or the Children's House.

12–1. Free games. 1–2. Directed games, if possible, in the open air.

The "children's house" was to be a real house, a set of rooms with a garden "of which the children are the masters." Montessori believed it important that the tables and chairs be sized for children, so that they might be easily moved around.

2–3. Manual work (clay modeling, etc.).
3–4. Collective gymnastics and songs, if possible in the open air.

The method provided a sharp contrast to stricter methods of education popular at the time, which kept children rule-bound and learning by rote. Montessori observed that, when left to their own devices, the children gravitated toward practical activities and the sharing of responsibilities. She saw self-discipline emerging in her charges: "It is frequently most touching to watch their efforts to imitate, to remember, and, finally, to conquer their difficulty." Her method is used around the world to this day.

 JANE ADDAMS

MATRON SAINT OF NEIGHBORS
B. 1860, UNITED STATES
Feast Day: September 6

The first orders of business were establishing a neighborhood reading group (they began with George Eliot) and setting up a kindergarten in one room of the dilapidated mansion. That mansion was Hull House, and its conversion to a settlement house—an inner-city institution aimed at providing social services to the community—was the brainchild of then-twenty-nine-year-old Jane Addams. Addams, who'd come from a wealthy family, had been inspired to social reform after reading Leo Tolstoy's *What Is to Be Done?* After visiting a London settlement house on a tour of Europe, Addams put up the initial funds for the project herself and, with her friend and partner, Ellen Gates Starr, established the settlement house in an area of Chicago that desperately needed it. "If it is natural to feed the hungry and care for the sick," she later wrote, "it is certainly natural to give pleasure to the young, comfort to the aged, and to minister to the deep-seated craving for social intercourse that all men feel." Within eight years of opening its doors, Hull House had been expanded into a thirteen-building complex; it occupied nearly an entire city block and included a theater, libraries, a post office, and a gymnasium. At its height, it received some two thousand visitors a week. Addams and the house's residents, mostly women, lobbied for women's rights, child labor laws, and the protection of immigrants. They succeeded in establishing the city's first public playground, as well. Addams's activism extended well beyond Hull House—she was a cofounder of the ACLU and the first American woman to win a Nobel Peace Prize—but she remained head resident at Hull House until her death, at the age of seventy-four.

✦ ELIZABETH I ✦

MATRON SAINT OF QUEENS
B. 1533, ENGLAND
Feast Day: September 7

*To me it shall be a Full satisfaction, both for the memorial of my
Name, and for my Glory also, if when I shall let my last breath, it be
ingraven upon my Marble Tomb, "Here lieth Elizabeth, which Reigned
a Virgin, and died a Virgin."*

—ELIZABETH I

The daughter of Henry VIII and Anne Boleyn was an unlikely
queen: after Boleyn was beheaded, young Elizabeth was declared
illegitimate. While under the rule of her half sister, Mary I—who
would go down as "Bloody Mary"—Elizabeth was imprisoned in the
Tower of London. But upon Mary's death, it was twenty-five-year-old
Elizabeth who succeeded to the throne, beginning a nearly forty-
five-year reign. Having inherited a bankrupt nation, under threat
from both France and Spain, she was pressured to create an international alliance through marriage. Instead, she managed to improve
England's relations with France, and her navy defeated the Spanish
Armada—all without a king. To the Parliament who'd expected her
to marry, she had this to say: "Now that the Publick Care of govern-
ing the Kingdom is laid upon me, to draw upon me also the Cares
of marriage may seem a point of inconsiderate Folly. Yea, to satisfie
you, I have already joyned myself in marriage to an Husband,
namely, the Kingdom of England."

 RUBY BRIDGES

MATRON SAINT OF FIRST STEPS
B. 1954, UNITED STATES
Feast Day: September 8

In 1960, *Brown v. Board of Education* was six years old, and so was Ruby Bridges, the first African American child to attend the all-white William Frantz Elementary School in New Orleans, amid the desegregation crisis. Bridges spent the whole first day in the principal's office; because of threats of poison, she was permitted to eat only food she'd brought from home. And young Bridges had to earn this dubious privilege, having been one of only six black children to pass an admissions test that was designed to be failed. At first only one teacher at the school, Barbara Henry, would agree to teach a black child, and Bridges became her sole student. (Decades later, after Bridges, who still lives in New Orleans, began her own foundation promoting tolerance in schools, the two were reunited on Oprah Winfrey's show.) Norman Rockwell dramatized Bridges's first day at Frantz in his painting *The Problem We All Live With*, but the photographs that survive from that November morning speak for themselves. There are throngs of white women, mothers who are pulling their children away from the school, and white boys, perhaps their sons. The women's mouths are open, shouting; a boy's sign reads, "All I Want for Christmas Is a Clean White School." Then there is small Ruby, carrying her schoolbag like a tiny briefcase, in those Mary Janes with the little white socks under them. Her head is down. She is minding her way down the school stairs. She comes up to the waist of the four U.S. marshals who escort her. Recalling the moment years later, one of the marshals said, "She just marched along like a little soldier."

MARIE CURIE AND IRÈNE JOLIOT-CURIE

MATRON SAINTS OF SCIENTISTS
B. 1867 AND 1897, POLAND AND FRANCE
Feast Day: September 12

In 1917, a factory in Orange, New Jersey, began producing watches that used radium-painted luminous faces, one of several companies to capitalize on the newfound popularity of the element. Some four thousand women became dial painters, even ingesting the radium as they wet the brushes with their tongues to refine the tip. Soon the health of these women began to fail. By the 1920s, they had begun to die of bone cancer. The "mother of modern physics," Marie Curie, must have been aware of the risks that came with exposure to radioactivity—on a trip to America, President Harding presented her with the gift of one gram of radium encased in a lead-lined box—but she didn't heed them, often working with bottles of the element in her coat pockets. Her research earned her two Nobel Prizes in Physics: one with her husband, Pierre, and another awarded to her alone. It also left her chronically ill and nearly blind of cataracts; the exposure ultimately led to her death, at the age of sixty-six, of aplastic anemia. Her work carried on without her, though, in the hands of her daughter Irène, who as a teenager began assisting her mother at field hospitals during World War I, setting up mobile radiology centers. Irène, along with her husband, Frédéric Joliot-Curie, succeeded in turning an element into another, radioactive element, thereby discovering induced radioactivity and winning her own Nobel Prize. Irène died of leukemia at only fifty-eight. Irène's own daughter, the nuclear physicist Hélène Langevin-Joliot, refutes the idea that her grandmother's life was sacrificed. "She did science because she wanted to," she said. "Because she loved research. That was of the utmost importance."

MARGARET SANGER

MATRON SAINT OF CHOICE
B. 1879, UNITED STATES
Feast Day: September 14

Two fires got Margaret Sanger to New York City: an actual house fire in the home she shared with her husband and children in the Hudson Valley, and her inner fire, the one that drove her to resume work as a nurse among immigrant communities in the Lower East Side. There she saw the effects that poverty and a lack of agency had on women: frequent childbirth, frequent miscarriages, and the often-tragic results of self-induced abortions. (Sanger knew something of these strains already: her own mother had endured eighteen pregnancies, of which eleven children had survived.) "When women gain their economic freedom they will cease being playthings and utilities for men," she wrote in 1912, in a series of columns aimed at mothers and girls. She later expanded on this idea: "The first step toward getting life, liberty, and the pursuit of happiness for any woman is her decision whether or not she shall become a mother. Enforced motherhood is the most complete denial of a woman's right to life and liberty." Sanger founded the nation's first birth control clinic, in Brooklyn, in 1916. She and her sister, Ethel Byrne, were arrested and convicted for distributing contraceptives, with one judge asserting that women did not have "the right to copulate with a feeling of security that there will be no resulting conception." Though her appeal failed, Sanger's trial won great publicity and many new donors for the cause. In 1921, Sanger founded the American Birth Control League. It is known today as Planned Parenthood.

 JUNKO TABEI

MATRON SAINT OF SUMMITS
B. 1939, JAPAN
Feast Day: September 22

If people want to call me "that crazy mountain woman," that's okay.

—JUNKO TABEI

That crazy mountain woman was the first female to scale Mount Everest. She was the first woman, too, to climb the Seven Summits—the highest peak on each continent. Mountaineering was not a woman's world back in the sixties, especially not in a country like Japan, where to this day women are required to assume their husband's last name. In the case of Junko Tabei (née Ishibashi), a future in mountain climbing seemed even less likely: she was the fifth of seven children, the daughter of a printer, a frail child who would never exceed four feet, nine inches in height. But where no path existed, Tabei blazed trails. "Some of the men wouldn't climb with me," she recalled. "Some thought I was there to meet men, but I was only interested in climbing." Ultimately, Tabei did marry a fellow climber—one who understood and supported her pursuit, working a stable job at Honda and looking after their children so she could chase higher and higher peaks. At thirty, she founded the Ladies Climbing Club: Japan (LCC), and the group she led up Everest was composed of herself and fourteen other women. After overcoming a dearth of funding for an all-women's climb, they were nearly stopped by an avalanche that wiped out their camp twelve days before reaching the top. When they made it, Tabei and the LCC were famous. Their slogan? "Let's go on an overseas expedition by ourselves."

DOROTHY ARZNER

MATRON SAINT OF MOTION PICTURES
B. 1897, UNITED STATES/RUSSIA
Feast Day: October 1

In 1975, Dorothy Arzner was honored by the Directors Guild of America. It was a long-overdue tribute to the golden-age film director—the guild's first female member—who helmed sixteen feature films and helped launch the careers of actresses including Lucille Ball and Rosalind Russell. Arzner was responsible for ensuring that Katharine Hepburn's second film role would be a strong one after seeing the actress around the studio: "She was about to be relegated to a Tarzan-type picture. I walked over to the set. She was up a tree with a leopard skin on!" Of her director, Hepburn later wrote, "She wore pants. So did I." Arzner, who was openly gay, wore not just pants but cuff links and tailored suits. She came to Hollywood a former premed student who'd joined the ambulance corps overseas during World War I. "I wanted to heal the sick and raise the dead instantly," she said of her career swap. "So that took me into the motion picture industry." Perhaps her background explains some of her technical ingenuity: filming silent star Clara Bow's first talkie, she rigged a microphone to a fishing rod, fashioning the first boom mike. Her most famous film, *Dance, Girl, Dance*, bombed at the box office but was later celebrated by first-wave feminist film critics for its empowered female characters and subversive challenge of the male gaze. The DGA's tribute came just four years before her death. At the ceremony, a telegram from Hepburn was read aloud: "Isn't it wonderful that you've had such a great career, when you had no right to have a career at all?"

ANNA POLITKOVSKAYA

MATRON SAINT OF THE BRAVE
B. 1958, UNITED STATES/RUSSIA
Feast Day: October 7

Two months before her death, journalist Anna Politkovskaya blends into a crowd of women, wearing a head scarf. The other women do their best to conceal her: it's important that she not be seen. A Chechen fighter, a man native to this village, has been killed on orders from the Kremlin. His head now hangs suspended from a gas pipeline, his bloodied track pants laid out below. It is summer, and the head has been out there for a while. The men in charge snap pictures with their cellphones. Then it is taken down—a small mercy—only to be sewn back onto its body and put on display again. A warning to Chechen adults, to their children, to whomever happens to be watching. Politkovskaya has been told that she mustn't be here—her reporting has made her enemies; there are threats on her life—but she is here, and she will write about what she sees.

Politkovskaya was born in New York, the daughter of diplomats. She could have chosen a life apart from this. She has already been arrested, poisoned, thrown into a pit. She has endured a mock execution at the hands of Russian troops. But as a journalist, she felt a duty to describe, as she put it, "the life around us for those who cannot see it for themselves." It was a duty that would cost her her life; in October 2006 she was found in an elevator in her Moscow apartment building, shot in the head and chest. Though it remains unclear who ordered the shooting, top-secret documents released by Edward Snowden confirm that Russian Federal Intelligence Services had targeted her email account. Two months before her murder, Politkovskaya wrote, "People in Chechnya are afraid for me, and I find that very touching. They fear for me more than I fear for myself, and that is how I survive."

THE NIGHT WITCHES

MATRON SAINTS OF THE SKY
EST. 1942, SOVIET UNION
Feast Day: October 8

Their pilot uniforms were hand-me-downs from their male counter-parts. Their planes were refurbished crop dusters, made of plywood and canvas, with open cockpits, without radios or radar. The aircraft could not even bear the added weight of parachutes. They flew in groups of two, these young Russian women, under cover of night. They were the 588th Night Bomber Regiment of the Soviet Air Forces, but German soldiers gave them the name *Nachthexen*, or "Night Witches," because the sound of their rickety planes was reminiscent of broomsticks clacking together. The Soviets were the first to use female pilots in combat roles, and in four years during World War II, the Night Witches dropped twenty-three thousand tons of bombs on Nazi invaders. "The Germans made up stories," one of the most famous of the regiment, Nadezhda Popova, later said. "They spread the rumor that we had been injected with some unknown chemicals that enabled us to see so clearly at night." In 2010, at the age of eighty-nine, Popova recalled, "I sometimes stare into the blackness and close my eyes. I can still imagine myself as a young girl, up there in my little bomber. And I ask myself, 'Nadia, how did you do it?'"

≫ HELEN HAYES ≪

MATRON SAINT OF THE STAGE
B. 1900, UNITED STATES
Feast Day: October 10

The Helen Hayes Theatre is the smallest theater on Broadway. It's a good fit for the star for whom the space was named, whose working-class Irish Catholic family nicknamed her "the white mouse." Hayes made her stage debut at the age of five. "I have always belonged to what I call the subway school of acting—that moving, roaring class-room where one studies fellow passengers," she wrote in her auto-biography. She worked on her voice and posture as well, becoming "the tallest five-foot woman in the world," and filled enormous shoes onstage, portraying Mary, Queen of Scots and Queen Victoria. In his review of *Mary of Scotland*, the *New York Times* theater critic wrote, "Slight as she is in stature (and Mary was six feet tall), Miss Hayes raises herself to queendom by the transcendence of her spirit." Hayes was a great star who insisted on downplaying the glamour of stardom, explaining her success in terms of her ap-proachability: "I seem always to have reminded people of someone in their family. Perhaps I am just the triumph of Plain Jane." The self-proclaimed plain Jane, the "mouse" of her family, was also the first woman to win an Emmy, Grammy, Oscar, and Tony—the elusive EGOT. (To date, only twelve individuals have won all four awards in competitive categories, among them Audrey Hepburn, Whoopi Goldberg, and Rita Moreno.) Still, she was foremost a stage actress—the "First Lady of the American Theater." When she died, at ninety-two, the marquee lights were dimmed all along Broadway.

ELEANOR ROOSEVELT

MATRON SAINT OF COMMON SENSE
B. 1884, UNITED STATES
Feast Day: October 11

"Eleanor, I hardly know what's to happen to you," Anna Rebecca Hall once told her young daughter, whose childhood looks earned her the nickname Granny. "You're so plain that you really have nothing to do except *be good*." Eleanor Roosevelt *was* good, though perhaps not in the way her mother had meant it. She was not just the longest-serving First Lady of the United States, but became the first chair of the United Nations Commission on Human Rights the year after. She went on to be declared the Gallup poll's most admired living woman, in 1948. In 1949 and 1950, too. Then in 1952, and 1953, and so on, uninterrupted through 1961. (The streak might have continued, had she not died the following year.) Much like her husband, Franklin, with his Fireside Chats, Eleanor had a particular way of establishing intimacy with the public: "My Day," her newspaper column, appeared six days a week, for an astonishing twenty-seven years. She wrote familiarly from her first entry, on New Year's Eve 1935: "I wonder if any one else glories in cold and snow without, an open fire within...all by one's self in one's own room?" (exhibiting shades of Virginia Woolf). Eleanor's column became a platform, too, for her political opinions—about race, the war, women's rights, education. In November 1960, she wrote, regarding the future of the country, "Whether you are a Republican or a Democrat, it seems to me this question of how we approach saving the world and its people from themselves is not a partisan question."

HILLARY CLINTON

MATRON SAINT OF POSSIBILITY
B. 1947, UNITED STATES
Feast Day: October 26

In 1969, a twenty-one-year-old Hillary Rodham delivered the commencement speech on behalf of her class at Wellesley College. "I find myself in a familiar position," she began, "that of reacting, something that our generation has been doing for quite a while now. We're not in the positions yet of leadership and power, but we do have that indispensable element of criticizing and constructive protest." Forty-eight years later, she returned to Wellesley, this time as a Clinton, a former First Lady, senator, and secretary of state, to speak to the graduating class of 2017. "Here's what I want you to know," she said, referring back to the year she graduated. "We got through that tumultuous time, and once again, we began to thrive as our society changed laws and opened the circle of opportunity and rights wider and wider for more Americans. We revved up the engines of imagination." At twenty-one, she had concluded her speech with an anecdote: "One of the most tragic things that happened yesterday, a beautiful day, was that I was talking to a woman who said that she wouldn't want to be me for anything in the world. She wouldn't want to live today and look ahead to what it is she sees, because she's afraid. Fear is always with us, but we just don't have time for it. Not now." Her message, at age sixty-nine, remained the same. "Your education gives you more than knowledge. It gives you the power to keep learning and apply what you know to improve your life and the lives of others," she said. "Get involved in a cause that matters to you. Pick one. Start somewhere. You don't have to do everything. But don't sit on the sidelines. And you know what? Get to know your elected officials. If you disagree with them, ask questions. Challenge them. Better yet, run for office yourself someday."

LISE MEITNER

MATRON SAINT OF DISCOVERY
B. 1878, AUSTRIA
Feast Day: October 27

At a Women's National Press Club dinner in 1946 honoring Lise Meitner, President Harry Truman darkly joked to the Austrian-Swedish physicist, "So you're the little lady who got us into all of this!" Throughout her tour of America that year, she was given celebrity treatment, as someone who'd "left Germany with the bomb in her purse." In fact, Meitner's contributions to the discovery of nuclear fission led Albert Einstein to write his famous letter of warning to President Franklin D. Roosevelt. In 1935, at the Kaiser Wilhelm Institute for Chemistry in Berlin, she had begun work alongside chemist Otto Hahn on a "transuranium research" program, which unexpectedly led to the discovery of nuclear fission three years later. By then, Meitner, a Jew, had already fled to the Netherlands, carrying with her a diamond ring—a gift from Hahn—in case the frontier guards demanded a bribe. Hahn, back in Germany, received the 1944 Nobel Prize in Chemistry, which many believed ought to have been shared with Meitner. But Meitner was concerned with far graver things than her own recognition. When invited to New Mexico to participate in the Manhattan Project, she declared, "I will have nothing to do with a bomb." And she never forgave Hahn and his associates for their "passive resistance" to Nazi Germany. "Millions of innocent human beings were allowed to be murdered without any kind of protest being uttered," she wrote in a letter to Hahn. "First you betrayed your friends, then your children in that you let them stake their lives on a criminal war—and finally you betrayed Germany itself."

 PUSSY RIOT

MATRON SAINTS OF PUNK
EST. 2011, RUSSIA
Feast Day: November 7

A mere forty seconds on February 21, 2012, changed the lives of the women of Pussy Riot, catapulting the Russian, feminist, punk-rock protest group to international fame. In brightly colored dresses and balaclavas, they took to the solea of an Orthodox church in Moscow and began to perform a protest song they referred to as a "punk prayer." The act was broken up by security, and two of the women were imprisoned, but video footage of the incident soon appeared on the Internet. (Sample lyrics: "Virgin Mary, Mother of God, banish Putin, banish Putin!") The arrests of these young women served to illustrate the very moral bankruptcy they were there to protest—the apparent dictatorship that had come to exist under the rule of President Vladimir Putin, and his regime's determination to silence his critics. A year later, Katya Samutsevich, one of Pussy Riot's more prominent members, appeared at the Sundance Film Festival—via video chat, following a screening of a documentary about the group. She was greeted with a theaterful of applause. When asked if they had any plans to officially release an album, Samutsevich answered no: "We reject commercialism of any sort, and we have no plans to release anything commercial. We will never commodify our art." Pussy Riot has continued to make new statements, more recently setting its sights on Donald Trump. During the run-up to the 2016 U.S. presidential election, the band released its own "Make America Great Again":

What do you want your world to look like?
What do you want it to be?
Do you know that a wall has two sides?
And nobody is free?

 LUCRETIA MOTT

MATRON SAINT OF SUFFRAGE
B. 1793, UNITED STATES
Feast Day: November 11

In the National Portrait Gallery in London, there hangs a painting by Benjamin Robert Haydon, nearly ten feet tall and twelve and a half feet wide. *The Anti-Slavery Society Convention, 1840* depicts a sea of pale faces hovering over black suits, with noted abolitionist Thomas Clarkson presiding. On the far right-hand side of the canvas, a cluster of attendees catches the eye, their white bonnets seeming to radiate light. Here are the women. The handful of female delegates sat segregated; the painting doesn't show it, but they were actually placed behind a screen. Among these women was Lucretia Mott, whose oration that week—calling for the rights of women—led the press to dub her "the Lioness of the Convention." Though they shared common enemies, many abolitionists did not welcome women to their cause, and so the women had to go off on their own. While there, Mott met and took under her wing a young Elizabeth Cady Stanton (who had come to the convention, of all places, on her honeymoon), and together the two assembled the first women's rights convention, held in Seneca Falls, New York. (On the convention's 150th anniversary, Hillary Clinton gave a speech, saying, "Much of who women are and what women do today can be traced back to the courage, vision, and dedication of the pioneers who came together at Seneca Falls.") Unlike Stanton, though, Mott welcomed the participation of men at the convention, and she made allies of such attendees as Frederick Douglass. "The speedy success of our cause," she determined, "depends upon the zealous and untiring efforts of both men and women." An account of the event, produced in Douglass's print shop, declared that Mott spoke with "her usual eloquence and power to a large and intelligent audience." She was "the moving spirit of the occasion."

JUANA INÉS DE LA CRUZ

MATRON SAINT OF INTELLECTUALS
B. 1651, MEXICO
Feast Day: November 12

God has given me the gift of a very profound love of truth.

—JUANA INÉS DE LA CRUZ

Like many female poets in history, Juana Inés de la Cruz never married, though she was renowned for her beauty and received several marriage proposals. Instead she became a nun—Sor Juana—using the convent of San Jerónimo y Santa Paula as a sanctuary for her education, the university in Mexico City being closed to women. She wished, she said, to have "no fixed occupation which might curtail my freedom to study." She became the convent's most famous member, entertaining intellectuals and conducting a type of salon. She filled her cell with books, artworks, and musical and scientific instruments. She wrote poems and essays that were published, and plays that were performed. After a while, though, her work began to get her in trouble with the church—her poetry was filled with lustful imagery, and her letters critiqued well-known sermons; she showed too great an interest in secular subjects. To this argument, Sor Juana replied, "One can perfectly well philosophize while cooking supper," and she signed one letter as "Me, the worst of all women." In response, the Catholic hierarchy cracked down. She lost her library—some four thousand volumes—and all her instruments of study. She was no longer permitted to publish. The church had been her sanctuary, but it was also her cage. A letter she wrote at the end of her life, directed to her critics, was published posthumously; it is regarded as a feminist manifesto of the New World. "Oh, how much injury might have been avoided in our land," she wrote, "if our aged women had been learned."

AUDRE LORDE

MATRON SAINT OF WORDS
B. 1934, UNITED STATES
Feast Day: November 17

She was born Audrey Geraldine Lorde, but even as a child she didn't like the *y* at the end of her name, its tail hanging down below the line. So she changed it. Born in New York, the daughter of Caribbean immigrants, she was so nearsighted that she was considered legally blind. In her youth, she memorized poems. "People would say, Well what do you think, Audre. What happened to you yesterday? And I would recite a poem and somewhere in that poem would be a line or a feeling I would be sharing." When she found no poem that expressed what she wanted to say, she began to write new ones herself; she was in the eighth grade. "Words had an energy and power," she said, "and I came to respect that power early. Pronouns, nouns, and verbs were citizens of different countries, who really got together to make a new world." When she found no words that expressed what she wanted to say, she created her own. During her years teaching in Berlin, she popularized the term "Afro-German," becoming an advocate for many black German women in their social and political development. She created the term "bio-mythography" to describe her book *Zami*, which had both "the elements of biography and history of myth," she wrote. "In other words, it's fiction built from many sources. This is one way of expanding our vision." Lorde, who described herself as a "black feminist lesbian mother poet," battled cancer at the end of her life and took on one more name, shortly before her death. In an African naming ceremony, she became Gambda Adisa. It means Warrior: She Who Makes Her Meaning Known.

⚛ WILMA MANKILLER ⚛

MATRON SAINT OF LEADERSHIP
B. 1945, CHEROKEE NATION
Feast Day: November 18

*Some people do earn their names in native culture. I didn't, but I
don't always tell people that. Sometimes I just say that Mankiller is my
name, I earned it, and I let 'em wonder.*

—Wilma Mankiller

On an early morning in November 1969, eighty-nine American Indians set out to lay claim to Alcatraz Island "in the names of Indians
of all tribes." The occupation lasted nineteen months, its participants
growing to four hundred strong, bringing federal Indian policy to
national attention—and to the attention of a twenty-four-year-old
wife and mother in Oakland. "What Alcatraz did for me was, it enabled me to see people who felt like I did but could articulate it
much better," Chief Wilma Mankiller later said. Ironically, Mankiller
might never have borne witness to the occupation—an experience
that, she wrote, "changed how I perceived myself as a woman and
as a Cherokee"—had her family not been part of the U.S. government's Relocation Act program of the 1950s, which moved them
from their Oklahoma farm to San Francisco. She would call it her
own little Trail of Tears.

Mankiller, after divorcing her husband, returned with her children to Oklahoma, where she became the first female chief of the
Cherokee Nation, tripling her tribe's enrollment, reducing its infant
mortality, and improving education. Mankiller, more soft-spoken
than many of the (male) council members, also installed a universal
off switch for the microphones, to thwart interruptions. She once
said, "Friends describe me as someone who likes to dance along the
edge of the roof. I try to encourage young women to be willing to
take risks, to stand up for the things they believe in." (For the record,
her favorite dancing song was Aretha Franklin's "Respect.")

⚞ BILLIE JEAN KING ⚟

MATRON SAINT OF CHAMPIONS
B. 1943, UNITED STATES
Feast Day: November 22

Any half-decent male player could defeat even the best female players.

—BOBBY RIGGS

I have often been asked whether I am a woman or an athlete. The question is absurd. Men are not asked that. I am a woman. I am an athlete.

—BILLIE JEAN KING

September 20, 1973. It was the largest live audience for a tennis match in U.S. history, with ninety million tuning in worldwide. Four months earlier, Riggs, a fifty-five-year-old former Wimbledon champion, had celebrated the defeat of former world No. 1 Margaret Court in a drubbing called the "Mother's Day Massacre." Now, Billie Jean King, who'd also ranked No. 1 in five previous years, had agreed to take him on. The match was billed as the Battle of the Sexes, and theatrics were high in the Houston Astrodome. King arrived Cleopatra-style, carried by bare-chested men, while her opponent rode in on a rickshaw drawn by almost equally underdressed women. King—who started out as a softball shortstop but whose parents pushed her into the more "ladylike" sport of tennis—won in three sets, hanging back by the baseline as Riggs tore around the court. Some people, upset at the victory, called foul: Riggs was twenty-five years older than King, the same age as her father. "For me to beat him meant absolutely nothing athletically," King later said. "Nothing. But it's what it represented." For King, who had just founded the Women's Tennis Association, crusading for equal pay for female tennis professionals, it represented a great deal. Title IX, an act that protected against discrimination on the basis of sex, had passed the year before. "It wasn't about a tennis match—it was about social change."

KARA WALKER

MATRON SAINT OF CONFRONTING HISTORY
B. 1969, UNITED STATES
Feast Day: November 26

A work of art was hung in the second-floor reference room of the Newark Public Library in New Jersey. It depicted the horror of Reconstruction, KKK figures beside a burning cross, Barack Obama orating behind a podium, and a black woman being forced to fellate a white man. It was on view for one day before the library director covered it with a zebra-print cloth. The staff had registered complaints. People were uncomfortable.

That was the point. When the piece—a six-by-nine-and-a-half-foot drawing titled *The Moral Arc of History Ideally Bends Towards Justice but Just as Soon as Not Curves Back Around Toward Barbarism, Sadism, and Unrestrained Chaos*—was unveiled once more, a local paper reported on it with an editor's note warning that "the artwork, which can be seen lower in this column, may be offensive to some readers." Several weeks after that, a group of more than one hundred people gathered for an hour in that public library; the artist, Kara Walker, had come to talk.

Walker was born in an integrated California suburb. When she was thirteen, the family moved to Georgia, where Walker learned that America was not as integrated as she'd thought. At her new school, she has said, "I was called a 'nigger,' told I looked like a monkey, accused (I didn't know it was an accusation) of being a 'Yankee.'"

Many of Walker's most celebrated pieces, black silhouettes on white backgrounds, take on a 360-degree circular format, literally surrounding the viewer. In one moment, the imagery is reminiscent of a storybook illustration; the very next, it is profoundly violent. Reflecting on the controversy, Walker has said, "If the work is reprehensible, that work is also me, coming from a reprehensible part of me. I'm not going to stop doing it, because what else could I do?"

ADA LOVELACE

MATRON SAINT OF GENIUS
B. 1815, ENGLAND
Feast Day: November 27

Ada Lovelace would not know her father, the poet Byron. Her mother, Annabella, made sure of that. Her parents were opposites that attracted and then repelled—the leader of Romanticism went from calling his mathematically inclined wife the "Princess of Parallelograms" to accusing her of being a "Mathematical Medea"—and Ada was diligently shielded from her father's influence. But she was still the daughter of art and science, as evidenced at an early age by her imagination. At twelve she began to investigate the mechanics of flight; she called it "flyology." (It is this inventive young Ada who would inspire Tom Stoppard's Thomasina, the brilliant character at the heart of his 1993 play *Arcadia*.) When Ada was seventeen, her mother took her to a party where she met the polymath Charles Babbage, who became her mentor. Babbage created the Analytical Engine, the first mechanical computer; Ada was the creation's interpreter. She saw the machine's potential to go beyond number crunching, that it could eventually process text, images, and music, and she articulated the significance of the invention better than its creator could. For this achievement, she is considered the first computer programmer. "Imagination," she wrote, "is the Discovering Faculty, pre-eminently. It is that which penetrates into the unseen worlds around us, the worlds of Science."

LOUISA MAY ALCOTT

MATRON SAINT OF SCRIBBLERS
B. 1832, UNITED STATES
Feast Day: November 29

Every few weeks she would shut herself up in her room, put on her scribbling suit, and "fall into a vortex," as she expressed it, writing away at her novel with all her heart and soul, for till that was finished she could find no peace.

The *she* here is Jo March, the heroine of Louisa May Alcott's most beloved novel, *Little Women*, but the author could just as well have been talking about herself. Like Jo, Alcott was the second of four daughters and the tomboy of the family. Alcott's descriptions of Jo writing offer insight not just into the author's self-perception but into her own struggles with her work. "With Spartan firmness, the young authoress laid her first-born on her table, and chopped it up as ruthlessly as any ogre. In the hope of pleasing every one, she took everyone's advice; and ... suited nobody." Learning to please oneself above all others was a privilege few women could afford. When Alcott's first novel, *Moods*, was published, she later wrote, "It was so altered, to suit the taste and convenience of the publisher, that the original purpose of the story was lost sight of." More notable than Alcott's similarities to her character, even, are their differences. Jo marries at twenty-five and has two children (leading to two sequels about her "little men"). Alcott, in her twenties, began writing for the *Atlantic Monthly*. During the Civil War, she worked as a nurse in a Union hospital, documenting her experience in an anti-slavery paper. She never married, though she did take in her late sister's daughter, another Louisa. And in 1882, almost twenty years after its publication, she returned to that first novel and restored its lost chapters. Alcott got the ending she wanted.

⇒ SHIRLEY CHISHOLM ⇒

MATRON SAINT OF FIRSTS
B. 1924, UNITED STATES
Feast Day: November 30

"Shirley Chisholm! What are you doing here?"

May 1972, a hospital room in Maryland. George Wallace, presidential hopeful, had just endured five hours of surgery following an assassination attempt—four bullets to the chest and stomach, one of them lodging in his spine—that would leave him paralyzed for the rest of his life. And though she was his opponent in the primary campaign, and though, as governor of Alabama, Wallace had once proclaimed, "Segregation now, segregation tomorrow, segregation forever," and though she was a black woman from Brooklyn—Shirley Chisholm showed up. Her whole life, Chisholm had been showing up: for child welfare, for the unemployed and disadvantaged, as the first black woman elected to the United States Congress (where she served seven terms), and as the first black woman to make a bid for the presidency (known for her slogan "Unbought and unbossed"). She often said she didn't want to be remembered for her candidacy in the presidential race. She knew she couldn't win. "I ran," she explained, "because somebody had to do it first." In the hospital that day, Wallace went on, asking, "What will your people say?" Her presence by his side would indeed cost her dearly at the polls. Chisholm didn't care. "I know what they are going to say," she told him. "But I wouldn't want what happened to you to happen to anyone."

THE GRIMKÉ SISTERS

In May 1838, as Angelina Grimké addressed a crowd in a Philadelphia hall, a mob was gathering outside in protest. Soon they were throwing rocks, shattering the windows. "Those voices without ought to awaken and call out our warmest sympathies. Deluded beings!" the younger Grimké sister said. "They know not that they are undermining their own rights and their own happiness, temporal and eternal." Angelina knew, as did her sister Sarah: they had been born, in South Carolina, to a wealthy family that owned more than one hundred slaves. As a girl, Sarah had been frustrated by the limited education she received, in contrast to her brothers', and horrified by the lashings of slaves she witnessed at the hands of her own family members. She found refuge up north, later returning for her sister, and the two devoted their lives to abolitionism. "As a southerner I feel that it is my duty to stand up here tonight and bear testimony against slavery.... I was brought up under its wing: I witnessed for many years its demoralizing influences, and its destructiveness to human happiness," Angelina said that day in Philadelphia. "I have *never* seen a happy slave. I have seen him dance in his chains, it is true; but he was not happy."

GRACE HOPPER

MATRON SAINT OF PROGRAMMERS
B. 1906, UNITED STATES
Feast Day: December 9

It looks like a class picture, the kind taken when one is very young—five in the back row, standing, and five in front, seated—only these are adults, in full U.S. Navy uniform. The year is 1944, and this is the original crew of Harvard's Mark I, the IBM Automatic Sequence Controlled Calculator. In other words: a computer, the size of a room. It looms behind them, extending well beyond the photo's frame. There is one woman in the picture, only one, hands folded in her lap—she has been issued a military skirt rather than pants—and her expression is the most somber of anyone's, her eyes trained on the camera lens. Grace Hopper arrived on the project as a junior-grade lieutenant, first in her class. She'd joined the Navy Reserve after Pearl Harbor but had been deemed too old—thirty-five—and too underweight—105 pounds—for military enlistment. (She would end her exceptionally long career as an admiral.) Right away, her colleagues were unwelcoming. "I later found out that they had been . . . trying to bribe each other as to which one would have the desk next to me," she recalled. Even those with whom she worked most closely reminded her that she "didn't know a computer from a tomato basket." But Hopper, who as a child had disassembled clocks to examine their machinery, learned quickly. Quickly enough to develop the first compiler, which could convert instructions into machine code, and to pioneer the use of human languages in programming, thereby opening the field up to those who didn't know machine code. In 2016, President Obama posthumously awarded Hopper the Presidential Medal of Freedom. In his words: "If Wright is flight, and Edison is light, then Hopper is code."

EMILY DICKINSON

MATRON SAINT OF VERSE
B. 1830, UNITED STATES
Feast Day: December 10

I picture her at Home
In simple White dress—
As if prepared Always for Sleep
Writing poems to Squirrel away
In a Drawer—
Under Lock and Key.

And perhaps this is the image she meant to leave us. Declining an invitation to a friend, at twenty-three: "I'm so old-fashioned, darling, that all your friends would stare." But Emily Dickinson was not, in fact, shy. At Mount Holyoke, she studied science and refused to be saved. When a teacher asked if she'd said her prayers, she answered yes, "though it can't make much difference to the Creator." With that, she was condemned to the category of "no-hopers." And though this major American female poet published little in her lifetime, she actively sought out professional connections. "Are you too deeply occupied to say if my Verse is alive?" she wrote to the literary critic Thomas Wentworth Higginson, who'd recently published an article of advice to young writers in the *Atlantic Monthly*. Her letter sparked a long correspondence between the two, though Dickinson declined his invitation to come to Boston ("I do not cross my Father's ground to any House or town"). Higginson ultimately came to meet her, in Amherst. Of the experience, he wrote, "I never was with any one who drained my nerve power so much. Without touching her, she drew from me. I am glad not to live near her."

⚛ ELLA BAKER ⚛

MATRON SAINT OF CIVIL RIGHTS
B. 1903, UNITED STATES
Feast Day: December 13

*Remember, we are not fighting for the freedom of the Negro alone,
but for the freedom of the human spirit, a larger freedom that encom-
passes all mankind.*

—ELLA BAKER

There is no national Ella Baker Day, and her name does not appear on standard-issue calendars across the country, but it is unlikely that Baker herself would have wanted the attention. The grand-daughter of slaves who graduated as valedictorian of her class, Baker played key roles in the Student Nonviolent Coordinating Committee and the NAACP–where, as branch director, she became its highest-ranking female member. In 1957, Dr. Martin Luther King, Jr., invited Baker to serve as executive director of his Southern Christian Leadership Conference. Baker accepted the role, but remained wary of any one leader becoming too central to the movement. "I think that, to be very honest, the movement made Martin rather than Martin making the movement," she said in an interview. "This is not to discredit him. This is, to me, as it should be." Baker herself advocated for group-centered leadership and focused on organization at the grassroots level. She helped register black voters, ultimately co-founding the Mississippi Freedom Democratic Party, an answer to the all-white Mississippi Democratic Party. She believed that voting was the one key to freedom. "You didn't see me on television, you didn't see news stories about me," she said. "The kind of role that I tried to play was to pick up pieces or put together pieces out of which I hoped organization might come. My theory is, strong people don't need strong leaders."

JANE AUSTEN

MATRON SAINT OF IRONY

B. 1775, ENGLAND

Feast Day: December 16

*I do not want people to be very agreeable, as it saves me the trouble
of liking them a great deal.*

—JANE AUSTEN

Jane Austen knew how to be wicked. So much so that very few of
her letters survive, her family having taken great pains, after her
death, to destroy or censor any comments they deemed too forth-
right. Surprising, then, how in recent years, professing a love for
Austen has become akin to professing oneself a romantic. The last
decade or two have seen an uptick not just in direct adaptations of
Austen's works but in novels and films depicting "Janeites"—avid
Austen fans who dream of forgoing their modern lives for entry
into the ideal worlds of her fiction. The misreading was something
Austen encountered even in her own day. In 1816, she wrote "Plan
of a Novel, According to Hints from Various Quarters," a brief par-
ody of the "ideal novel," written in response to suggestions she'd
received from readers of her work. In it, the Heroine—"a faultless
character herself, perfectly good, with much tenderness and senti-
ment, and not the least Wit"—meets with the Hero, who is "only
prevented from paying his addresses to her by some excess of re-
finement." Later the Heroine's ailing father, a clergyman, "after 4 or 5
hours of tender advice and parental Admonition to his miserable
Child, expires in a fine burst of Literary Enthusiasm." In a surviving
letter to her niece, she wrote, "Pictures of perfection, as you know,
make me sick."

FAITH SPOTTED EAGLE

MATRON SAINT OF ACTIVISTS
B. 1948, YANKTON SIOUX NATION
Feast Day: December 19

The six weeks following the 2016 United States presidential election saw a renewed interest in the 538 electors who would cast their votes in the indirect election established by the Twelfth Amendment to the Constitution. Seven electors declined to vote for the presidential candidates to whom their states were pledged, casting "faithless ballots" on December 19, 2016—a historic number, previously exceeded only in cases where a candidate was no longer living. One of those votes, from an elector in Washington State, went to Faith Spotted Eagle, marking the first time an electoral vote went to a Native American (and, along with Hillary Clinton, the first two instances when an electoral vote went to a woman). "I thought it was fake news," Spotted Eagle later told a reporter. "I told my daughter, 'Is this real?' She said, 'I think it is.'" Spotted Eagle has a history of activism, having protested the Vietnam War and helped to create the first Native American women's shelter. Now, as a "grandmother"—a wise female elder—she has been a leader in the victories against the construction of the Dakota Access Pipeline, which would transport half a million barrels of crude oil a day through sacred grounds. On CNN, she compared the plan to building a pipeline through Arlington National Cemetery. Speaking of her time in the protest camps, she said, "I think it's a rebirth of a nation, and I think that all of these young people here dream that one day they would live in a camp like this, because they heard the old people telling the stories of living along the river.... They're living the dream."

MARGARET HAMILTON

MATRON SAINT OF ENGINEERS
B. 1936, UNITED STATES
Feast Day: December 21

It was just supposed to be a job to help pay the bills while her husband finished law school. Their young daughter would have to come to the lab with her. The year was 1960, and her colleagues at MIT were mostly men. (They didn't bring their children to work.) Their team was tasked with the job of coding the first portable computer. With only an undergraduate degree in mathematics, Hamilton distinguished herself as a problem solver, and she was soon tapped by NASA. By 1965, she was responsible for all the onboard flight software on Apollo computers. Her daughter, Lauren, was still coming to the lab with her on nights and weekends. It was Lauren who, fiddling with a keyboard, crashed the command simulator, inspiring Hamilton to add error-checking code to the software that no one considered necessary. Five days into the flight of *Apollo 8*, an astronaut accidentally triggered the same error Lauren had. It was Hamilton's code that brought the spacecraft home. "Looking back," Hamilton has said, "we were the luckiest people in the world; there was no choice but to be pioneers; no time to be beginners."

LOUISE BOURGEOIS

MATRON SAINT OF THE AVANT-GARDE
B. 1911, FRANCE
Feast Day: December 25

God worked six days and rested on the seventh. Louise Bourgeois, into her nineties, worked six days, and on the seventh, she held a salon in her home, critiquing the work of young artists. The forum came to be known by its participants as Sunday, Bloody Sunday; Bourgeois pulled no punches. In one such session, while manipulating a piece of clay, she explained her early leap from painting to sculpting: "When you go from painting to this, it means you have an aggressive thought.... [Sculpting] allowed me to express what I was embarrassed to express before." She is said to have then wrung the neck of the figure in her hands. For all her severity, the toughest, most unflinching elements of Bourgeois's work look back to her girlhood: her father's betrayals of her mother and a shadowy conception of sex that left her feeling vulnerable. In 1968 she produced a two-foot-long latex phallus and called it *Fillette,* French for "little girl." She posed, for Robert Mapplethorpe, with it tucked like a handbag under her arm. And one of her most iconic pieces, an imposing thirty-five-foot spider made of bronze, stainless steel, and marble that was first displayed at the Tate Modern, she titled *Maman* ("Mommy"). "Spiders are friendly presences that eat mosquitoes," she has said. "We know that mosquitoes spread diseases and are therefore unwanted. So, spiders are helpful and protective, just like my mother."

MARLENE DIETRICH

MATRON SAINT OF GOING OFF-SCRIPT
B. 1901, GERMANY
Feast Day: December 31

She had just a minute with a hot microphone to say whatever she wanted. She was in North Africa, delivering a radio broadcast for the Armed Forces Network. She'd been asked to sing "Lili Marlene," a popular wartime song that had been banned by the Nazi government's propaganda minister. As soon as she went off-script, she'd be stopped. She forged ahead anyway, speaking quickly in her native German: "Boys! Don't sacrifice yourselves! The war is shit! Hitler is an idiot!" As expected, the army announcer took her microphone away—this was a broadcast for *American* troops. Still, she felt sure, German troops would hear it on "black" radio stations set up by the U.S. government's Morale Operations Branch. Hitler had wanted Marlene Dietrich for Germany; Nazi agents had tried to bribe her to return from Hollywood. Instead, the Berlin-born star of *The Blue Angel* and *Shanghai Express* became an American citizen in 1939, and as World War II began, she started war-bond drives and a fund for Jewish refugees. In 1943, she left Hollywood and traveled overseas to perform with the USO. One veteran remembered her visit to a Red Cross hospital in Naples: after a performance in the dining hall, Marlene "began a relentless, seven-day, dawn-to-dusk tour of the entire hospital.... You can be certain that I became and remain an avid fan, loyal to the memory of Marlene Dietrich—the lady who laughed at Hitler, refused his command appearance order and poured body and soul into the World War II effort." Dietrich, for her part, would always refer to that time in her life as "the only important thing I've ever done."

YOUR OWN FEMINIST SAINT

‡ _____ ‡

NAME

_____

MATRON SAINT OF

_____

BIRTH YEAR AND HOMELAND

_____

FEAST DAY

_____

_____

_____

_____

_____

_____

_____

_____

_____

_____

_____

_____

_____

_____

_____

ACKNOWLEDGMENTS

I want to thank, as always, Elyse Cheney. I am grateful to have found such a wonderful collaborator in Manjit Thapp. This book would not exist without the brilliant Caitlin McKenna. You can't put anything past her.

—Julia Pierpont

Thank you, Mum, for your endless support, and Laura, for all the times we drew in class. I would also like to thank Caitlin McKenna for making this whole process a complete dream, and Julia Pierpont for your compelling biographies. They were a joy to illustrate.

—Manjit Thapp

And a big thank-you to everyone who contributed names. Your passion inspired us: Alex Henry, Alex Kondo, Alwa Cooper, Andra Miller, Angela McNally, Anna Pitoniak, Ashleigh Heaton, Ben Stark, Betsy Cowie, Brenden Beck, Caitlin Endyke, Caroline Calkins, Casey Selwyn, Cindy Spiegel, Claudia Roth Pierpont, Dain Goding, Daria Solomon, Dennis Ambrose, Emi Ikkanda, Erica Gonzalez, Erika Hval, Grace Kallis, Hannelore McKenna, Jane Zimmer, Janet Glazier, Jean Carbain, Jen Garza, Jennifer Rice, Jennifer Rodriguez, Nina Rouhani, Jessica Henderson, Josh Brechner, Kaela Myers, Kaley Baron, Katie Okamoto, Kesley Tiffey, Lindsay Adkins, Loren Noveck, Lucy Silag, Maggie Yolen, Matt Burnett, Melanie DeNardo, Michael McKenna, Michelle Jasmine, Mika Kasuga, Molly Turpin, Morgan McKenna, Porscha Burke, Robbin Schiff, Robert Pierpont, Sabine Zimmer, Sarah Beth, Sarah Locke, Sharanya Durvasula, Shauna Summers, Sheila Lawton, Steve Messina, Susan Corcoran, Susan Kamil, Ted Allen, Toby Ernst, Tricia Narwani, Victory Matsui, and Vincent La Scala.

ABOUT THE AUTHOR

JULIA PIERPONT is the author of the *New York Times* bestseller *Among the Ten Thousand Things*, the winner of the Prix Fitzgerald in France. She is a graduate of Barnard College and the MFA program at New York University. Her writing has appeared in *The Guardian*, *The New Yorker*, *The New York Times Book Review*, and *Guernica*. She lives and teaches in New York.

Twitter: @juliapierpont

ABOUT THE ILLUSTRATOR

MANJIT THAPP is an illustrator from the United Kingdom. She graduated with a BA in illustration from Camberwell College of Arts in 2016. Her illustrations combine both traditional and digital media, and her work has been featured by Instagram, *Dazed*, *Vogue India*, and *Wonderland* magazine.

Instagram: @manjitthapp

ABOUT THE TYPE

This book was set in Nofret, a typeface designed in 1986 by Gudrun Zapf-von Hesse especially for the Berthold foundry.

grace maya . oprah kitty

amelia frances * billie bella

anne . del . Katharine * gloria

patria sandra · ada . mari

lise dolores * margaret hilla

sappho · marlene * cecile

kara . charlotte * elizabeth

lucretia * jin eleanor · dor

virginia mae faith dorothea

erma nadezhda nellie ire

michelle · jane ruby * marga

maria phyllis * harriet h

kasha · maria teresa· phillis

maya* oprah kitty ida